NANTUCKET BEACH PICNICS
A Cookbook * A Scrapbook * A Guide

By Deborah Moxham and Carla Finn

Deborah Moxham and Carla Finn
Nantucket Beach Picnics
28 John Street
Providence RI 02906
401 831 7500

Photographs:
Janet D. Alcott
William Bassell
John M. Clark
Carla Finn
Robert Finn
Brian Jones
Deborah Moxham

Printed in the United States of America
First edition

Book Design:
nickynichtern.com

DEDICATION

From Deborah

For my mother, Sidney Mitchell Todd Moxham,
who has given me so much, including Nantucket.

From Carla

For Rob, Heather and Bob, who helped
me with computer problems, testing recipes,
and taking beach pictures, and gave me the
support I needed to make this happen.

TABLE OF CONTENTS

Foreword 6

Introduction 7

Planning 11

    The Necessities 13

    Clean Up 14

Nantucket Beach Information 16

Picnic Beaches 18

Early Memories 20

Recipes 28

    Appetizers: Dips, Soups, and Hors d'oeuvres 29

    Salads 53

    Brunch and Teatime 73

    Meat, Poultry, and Vegetarian Entrées 87

    Seafood Entrées 125

    Side Dishes 139

    Desserts 165

    Cocktails 191

Saying Goodbye.. 211

Conclusion 213

About the Authors 214

Index.. 217

For as long as we can remember, Nantucket has been a part of our lives. We both have early childhood memories of the island, and we have both had the distinct privilege of offering our own children Nantucket summers and falls and winters. Over the years, we have each had our own separate lives and friends, but we have shared a core group of friends with whom we have met many of life's passages. This book sprang from the happiness and fun we have had with our friends, from the meals we have shared, from the sunsets, the bonfires, the recipes, and the memories.

We want to thank those friends, each and every one of them, and give this back to them and to you as our gift. We believe "a recipe that is not shared with others will soon be forgotten, but when it is shared, it will be enjoyed for future generations." We know that our friends will appreciate our finally getting these recipes down on paper after so many promises, and we hope that our own children will not only use them but be able to conjure up the memories that accompany them.

Deborah

Nantucket is a feast for the senses. First, the eyes take in the natural beauty of the moors and the sweeping beaches, then the charm of the cobblestone streets and gray-shingled houses with their crisp white trim. Familiar sounds abound, soothing and reassuring—the song of the fog horn or the rattle of the screen door, the cry of the gulls swooping over the harbor, three blasts of the ferry horn as it slips from its berth and turns toward the mainland. The smell of roses and privet infuses the air, and most Nantucketers returning home are reminded of the distinctive smell of houses that sit by the sea. There is the sensation of fog so thick it wets your eyelashes, wind in your hair, sun on your skin, and sand between your toes. Finally, it's taste, and whether it's the sweetness of the summer corn or the glory of the tomatoes, a dinner at one of the local eateries or on a friend's wharfside porch, the taste buds are tickled.

The most wonderful way to combine all the senses is a Nantucket beach picnic, out at one of the South Shore beaches, watching the sun fade into orange and the moon begin its climb. As the waves roll on shore, immense beauty washes over you. Over the past quarter-century, our small group of friends has had hundreds of beach picnics, beginning when our children were young and our parents were the age we are now. We have had our own fireworks, when one of the fathers brought home treasures from Hong Kong. We have collected baby conch purses and chased the moonlit phosphorous washing onto the North Shore. We have roasted thousands of marshmallows near Long Pond and watched fishermen haul sharks onto the beach at Esther Island. We have seen the full moon rise above the Great Point Lighthouse and sat around our fire counting the stars shooting across the August sky.

Our group grows and shrinks as the years go by, filled with laughing children who become friends by association and proximity and grandparents who come because they remember their own picnics. But all along, the same families have been there, loving Nantucket, growing older together. Carla Finn is the backbone of these picnics, providing a continuum of organization and a panoply of creative twists. I can't even remember a time when I did a picnic without Carla. We actually met on the beach. We met when our children were five years old, and we had signed them up for swimming classes at the jetties.

In retrospect, we realize what a sadistic enterprise it was, in early June when the water was freezing and the air usually filled with fog. We sent them in again and again, blue lipped and shivering, because learning to swim was an essential requirement for Nantucket summers and because we were having fun getting to know each other, bundled in our sweatshirts on the beach. We hadn't known each other long before we decided to have a beach picnic so that we could introduce our husbands and make it an evening event with great food.

We like to think our beach picnics are sensational. Back then, they were just hamburgers and hot dogs, but they have evolved to include much more sophisticated fare. We always arrive with a number of treats we can set out immediately to nibble on while the grills are being fired up and the chairs assembled. It's tough to hold back on our hors d'oeuvres and leave room for dinner, but it's worth it because the meals we cook are great in themselves, and besides, everyone knows nothing ever tastes better than it does in the great outdoors.

Needless to say, we had to learn how to carry off a completely successful beach picnic. Some of the early ones were much more work because we didn't have a system. There were times when we were sandblasted by winds blowing off the sound or rained on in 'Sconset when it was dry on the North Shore. We have been to beaches so crowded we had to angle for a parking spot as though it were the Stop and Shop. There were picnics when we were skimpy on entrées and overloaded with salads and desserts, and others when the food got so soggy in the fog it was inedible.

We have learned to scope out the weather and let our telephones do the planning, and all this has resulted in an impressive display of precision operations that get us from backdoors to beach chairs in record time. We have learned how to plan for food that keeps the picnic moving and makes the grilling almost an anticlimax. We know what essentials to have on hand, what drinks work for a crowd, and, worst of all, how to pack it up and take it home. We know the best beaches and the sweetest secret spots. We have it down to a science, and we are going to save you the learning curve and also give you our most successful recipes.

TIPS FOR DRIVING ON THE BEACH

* Always carry a shovel and a board in your vehicle. If you get stuck, you should dig out the area around the stuck tire and then put the board under it, which will help you drive out of the area. Never spin your tires because that only digs you in deeper. You can always let more air out of the tire.

* Never drive or park too near the water or in soft sand.

* Stay in the proper lanes. Courtesy is the name of the game on the beach as there are no stop signs or stop lights. Always try to stay in the proper inbound and outbound lanes, and when passing a vehicle on the beach, do not get too close as beach driving is sometimes quite uneven.

* Drive at a reasonable speed. There are always dogs and children to watch out for.

* Drive caravan style. When you go out to Great Point with several different cars, it is nice to make a caravan going back at night to make sure everyone gets in safely.

LOCATION

Once we settle on a day for a picnic, we need to be on top of the wind direction before we pick a beach. If the wind is coming from the South, the North Shore beaches are the most sheltered, and vice versa. If it is relatively calm, then all the beaches are a possibility, and we make our choice according to everyone's schedule. Sunday nights are a great choice because so many of the husbands leave early Monday morning, and it is a quiet way to end a weekend. Nantucket is such a busy place that nearly every Friday and Saturday night of the summer, there are exciting events and tempting invitations. But Sunday is family night, and if it ends up on the sand watching the sunset and lighting a bonfire to stretch out the moonrise, it has a tranquil and sweet effect on everyone. If we feel adventurous, we will make the trek to Great Point, where the moon behind the lighthouse is particularly intoxicating. With water all around and fishermen silhouetted in the fading light, the magic abounds. Quite often, however, we head out to the South Shore to a little beach near Tristram's Landing, which so far has been exclusively ours. Finding privacy on a Nantucket beach is easier than one would guess, and we are almost always successful. Someone always has a four-wheeler available to ferry people over the sand to 40th Pole or out to Great Point, and more often than not, there are several four-wheelers available.

THE FOOD

The word *picnic* did not originally refer to outdoor meals but to meals in which guests contributed the dishes—that is, they were like potlucks. It was in Victorian times that the term became linked with open-air dining. That is basically what our beach picnics are—potluck open-air dinners.

The way we arrange our picnics never varies. Each participating family brings their own drinks and main course, and we divvy up the hors d'oeuvres and side dishes and desserts among ourselves. It seems everyone brings at least one appetizer and side dish, so we have a veritable smorgasbord to choose from. Desserts can be as simple as brownies, but for the kids and the adult Peter Pans, we generally have s'mores available. The ritual alone makes them appealing and justifies keeping that fire going.

DON'T FORGET YOUR...

Coolers—one solely for clean ice for drinks
Plastic cups
Plastic or paper plates
Napkins
Salt, pepper, condiments
Paper towels
Utensils
Tools: spatula, large fork, good knife, corkscrew,
        can opener
Cutting board
Skillet
Potholders
Aluminum foil
Clear garbage bags
Metal bucket
Tables—one for every six people
Tablecloths with clothespins
Beach chairs—one per adult
Blankets
Beach towels
Grills—one for every six adults
Charcoal—instant-light preferable, or bring a charcoal
            chimney to speed the process
Matches
Outdoor candles
Not imperative but a big plus: a wire brush to clean the
hot grill and containers for leftovers

THE NECESSITIES

Everyone brings a cooler, and everyone brings ice. We keep some ice in the bags to make sure we have clean ice for drinks. Our standard-issue picnic basket includes plastic cups, paper or plastic plates, napkins, paper towels, and utensils, including a spatula, a large fork, and a sharp knife. These things are always in the basket and returned to it after each use. It is important to bring potholders, a box of aluminum foil for covering food, and plenty of garbage bags and a metal bucket for cleanup. Matches and a lighter are necessary for the charcoal—instant light charcoal is the easiest. Wet wipes are always welcome, and it is important to have a flashlight or lantern for cleaning up in the dark and looking for that inevitably lost sandal.

We always bring at least one folding table, with a tablecloth and clothespins to hold it in place. Beach chairs are a must for adults and teenagers, but most kids are happy with a blanket. Beach towels are good to have along as someone always wants to take an early evening dip. When the group exceeds six people, we bring along another table, and the number of grills goes up as well.

We usually get the grills started almost as soon as we arrive, especially if we are using regular charcoal. With the instant-light charcoal, this is not such a pressing issue as the fire is ready in 12 minutes.

We try to arrive at the beach at a specific time. This way, all hands are on deck to haul the supplies over the dunes. If we are driving right onto the beach, then obviously it is a short jump from tailgate to table, but if we are parked on the other side of the dune, it usually means three or four trips for each person ferrying in the tables, chairs, and food.

The first people to arrive at the beach set up the tables and get out the drinks. In our case, we hand glasses of our own secret-formula Planter's Punch to each hauler, and it goes down so fast that people are cheerful by the last trip back and forth to the car.

PERMITS

The Nantucket Fire Department requires a permit for outdoor grilling. In 2006, the annual permit costs $5 a year, and senior citizens get one free.

The permit entitles you to have a charcoal or propane grill on any beach on the island. Quite often, homeowners buy one for their house and their renters, but you must have it on you when you go to the beach to have a cookout.

CLEAN UP

CLEAR garbage bags
One for throwaway
One for recycling
One for dirty, non-throwaway items, like plates, silver-ware, and plasticware worth saving.

We always put the trash in one big car and go through it before it goes to the dump. There is always something accidentally tossed, and the clear bags make it easy to find.

Keep one cooler or basket separate for storing all the items you need at every picnic. These items should be washed and put right back into that container so you never need wonder whether there is a spatula (turning hamburgers with fingers is dicey) or a saltshaker or matches.

Charcoal:
When the fires burn down, there is the problem of the embers. Burying them under sand is not safe as the fire can stay warm and some unsuspecting beachcomber might walk on the hot sand. What we always do: soak the embers with seawater and then scoop them into a metal bucket to dispose of at home. This is the best way to cut down on litter and the destruction of the beaches.

BEACHES WITH LIFEGUARDS

Children's Beach
Jetties Beach
Dionis Beach
Madaket Beach
Cisco Beach
Miacomet Beach
Surfside Beach
'Sconset Beach

DRIVING ON BEACHES:

Each year the sands shift around the island with some eroding and others building up. As a result there is an annual decision made to determine which beaches are safe to drive on.

This is the list for 2006 for four wheel drive vehicles:

* Between Cisco and Miacomet
* Dionis (40th Pole)
* Fisherman's Beach
* Nobadeer
* Surfside
** Coatue
** Great Point

In order to drive on the first five beaches, you must purchase a permit from the Police Department for $100 (good for one year).

** Require a separate permit which is available at the Wauwinet Gate House. Fee: $100 for cars registered on Nantucket and $125 for cars registered off-island.

16

NANTUCKET BEACH INFORMATION

Washing Pond Beach:
Lovely, fairly secluded. A short walk over the dunes to the beach. Beware of soft sand in parking areas, which are located off Washing Pond Road.

Jetties Beach:
A great little snack bar, rest rooms, boardwalk, outdoor showers, calm waters, swings, and great beach walking.

Children's Beach:
Right in town, perfect for toddlers, nearby restaurant, swing sets and slides, and Sunday night band concerts.

Dionis Beach:
Rest rooms, lifeguard, great beach walking.

Steps Beach:
Great spot away from the crowds, but you must carry your gear up and down about 50 steps that lead from the Cliff to the beach.

40th Pole:
A favorite of local Nantucketers, accessed only by four wheel drive. Walk to Eel Point and look for shells.

Eel Point

Smith Point

Madaket P

Sheep's Pond Beach:
Our secret spot for picnics, accessed through Tristram's Landing.

Cisco Beach P

Fat Ladies Beach:
For years, our favorite place for taking our kids to a surf beach and seeing friends.

Naked Beach:
Nude sunbathing.

Miacomet:
Great for surf or pond swimming, and perfect for an evening get together.

Coatue: Accessible only by boat or car. Lots of soft sand, so tire pressure of 12 psi is recommended. Plenty of opportunities for privacy, great swimming, beautiful conservation land.

Brant Point Beach: Easy walking and biking distance from town and great for viewing the harbor hubbub.

Great Point: Our favorite picnic destination when we have time for the journey. Dangerous cross rip at the point, so don't even think about swimming in this location. Swim on the harborside, and picnic by the lighthouse. Aim for a full moon.

Pocomo Point: At head of harbor - great for a picnic or a swim. Look down toward Nantucket town and see every boat in the harbor.

Wauwinet: Get your stickers here at the Gate House for Great Point and Coatue.

Quidnet Beach: Lovely little hamlet perfect for picnics. You can swim in Sesachacha Pond or the ocean and have a sheltered picnic at either pond or the ocean.

'Sconset Beach: For picnics we go to the end of Codfish Park, which is down the hill from the Sconset Rotary.

Low Beach: Absolutely beautiful beach with wild look because of the winds and the open sea, but swim only with a lifeguard on duty.

Surfside Fisherman's Nobadeer

These three beaches are the hot spots for teenagers and young people, probably because you can easily take a shuttle from town, and there are great sandbars for swimming.

Madaquecham: Georgeous stretch of beach accessed through rolling moors. Another favorite with the kids but plenty of opportunity to find your own private spot.

Tom Nevers Beach: Dangerous rip here, with a big drop off, so swimming here should never be done unaccompanied. It makes a lovely picnic spot however.

There are many great beaches on which you may not drive, but you can still have a lovely picnic. The plus is that you don't have to let the air out of your tires; the minus is that you do have to carry all of your gear onto the beach.

The South Shore beaches stretch for seven miles, and some of the non-driving beaches are perfect for sunset picnics. One of our favorite spots is still a well-kept secret. It is a lovely stretch of beach out in the Sheep Pond area. To get there, you must take the Madaket Road out to Tristram's Landing, turning left at that sign. Go down the road, cross over a little bridge, and bear right. Continue on until the road divides and stay on the right. Follow the road around through several bends. At the final right-hand bend, there will be a house on your left. (It will be the only house that is next to the road). After you pass that house on the left, your next left-hand turn will be into the parking area for your picnic destination.

There is also another nice spot out in this same area, and we refer to this one as Tristram's. Again, head out the Madaket Road and turn in at Tristram's Landing. After you go over the little bridge, do not bear to the right but continue on straight, and you will eventually come to a parking area with the ocean on the right and a small pond on the left.

Another highly recommended beach is out by the Miacomet Golf Club. Take Hummock Pond Road until you see the left-hand turn for the Miacomet Golf Course. Continue on past the club on your left, and you will come to the beach. Miacomet Pond is the very large pond that will be on your left. Four-wheel drive vehicles were once permitted on this beach after 5:00 p.m., but it is no longer accessible.

We have had several nice beach picnics out in 'Sconset at the Codfish Park Beach. This is a nice wide beach and great for a crowd. The last time we were there was for a birthday party, and it was very misty and foggy, which added tremendous ambiance.

Out in Quidnet, you have your choice of picnicking either at the Sesachacha Pond or by the ocean. We have most often set up by the pond. Our children had great times on that pond with a huge float they called "Great Island."

We have great memories of summer times in Quidnet with the children playing flashlight tag or having lemonade stands, so staging a picnic there is always popular.

There is a nice public access at the end of Pocomo, which is off the Wauwinet Road. This spot is a popular gathering point for sailboarders. That might mean great spectating, but it also might make for a congested picnic setup. If you do choose Pocomo, you'll find it a perfect place to find good seashells.

40th Pole Beach is a favorite North Shore spot with local Nantucketers. You find it by driving out the Eel Point Road past most of the houses. On your right, you will see a telephone pole with the number 40 on it. Turn into a small parking area, which often has several cars in it. Head in past the cars and drive right over the dunes in the worn tire tracks. Once you reach the shore, turn left, and you can drive as far as you want. This beach has great sandbars, calm waters, and plenty of sheltering dunes.

As we mentioned, Great Point is a magic spot, but it does require a time commitment of several hours. Getting there and back takes at least 90 minutes. It is possible, however, to head for Great Point and take your first left onto Coatue. Coatue has five points of beaches that are lovely and secluded, with calm harbor swimming. Beware of one thing, however. The beaches are very soft, and even veteran drivers can get stuck along the way.

EARLY MEMORIES

Deborah

My grandfather introduced me to Nantucket, and all of these years later, the memories are distinct and sharp. I regularly recall driving in his jeep from his Easton Street home to an early-morning Main Street visit to the Hub or the post office. We would make the rounds on much quieter streets, stopping at Stinky's (a.k.a. Stinchfield's), his favorite clothing store. Such a natty dresser, Grandpa would pick up a colorful sports jacket with a checkered lining and a checkered bow tie to match. We'd ride out the Cliff Road to a shack where Madaket Millie was then selling ice cream. I have no idea why or for how long she did that, but my Grandpa would get those big commercial containers of butterscotch royal or chocolate to store in his freezer. We'd go to Murray's, all of them, and Miriam Congdon's and the Mad Hatter. At night my sister and I would ride our bikes to the Dreamland. With Grandpa we would fish and sail and go to Coatue, where he would pop corn in an old basket popper over the fire, and we'd run out to jump off the dock before the horseflies could get us. Those same summers, my parents would be renting the boathouse next door, now a lovely place owned by Nelson Doubleday. But then, it was like a big old barn, and they had all these glamorous friends from Broadway, like Jerome Robbins and Sonny Simone, and they would be practicing high kicks and dancing the night away.

My memories are bright and happy, as Nantucket always seems. As I grew up, I started spending summers on Long Island, sailing and swimming and having fun. But when I came back to Nantucket for a weekend in my twenties, I longed to return. So, there I was, being married by Ted Anderson on Christmas Day in the basement of the church where my grandparents had married in 1918. Soon, we were renting a house each summer, and finally we had our own place. I remember my daughter eating her first strawberry—an amazing and exciting discovery—from the farm truck on Main Street and my own children visiting the Hub for Archie Comics and going to the Dreamland.

Always fun, always interesting people, like Mr. Constable with his beautiful blue eyes, or Michael Shannon at the Club Car, who cooked the enormous mushroom my daughter found in our backyard, or Harbormaster Ken Lapin, who lived next door and rescued my daughter at one in the morning when she was stuck in the sand at a party and who took my dad to the hospital at night when he tripped over one of the girls' bicycles. I loved spending time with Roy Bailey at his studio and meeting the people who trickled in during the day for a piece of Roy and a laugh. Every summer, I looked forward to seeing Chick Walsh when I had dinner at my favorite restaurant on the planet, and I still prefer seeing Mimi Beman at Mitchell's—she can tell me what I'll want to read far better than any automated database on Amazon. There were always great events, like Jimmy Barker's gallery lunches for celebrity guests and artists, or Bud and Wink Gifford's annual summer cocktail parties, my parents' 50th anniversary on a harborside lawn, or my own 50th birthday party at our house on Vestal Street.

Selling that house and losing my toehold on Nantucket were painful indeed, but it is remarkable to realize that those memories are rich and strong and will always belong to me.

Deborah

My early memories of Nantucket are of my grandparents, Jim and Betty Todd, and their wonderful Brant Point house. My grandfather had inherited the house from his mother, who inherited it from my great-great-grandparents. My parents had married on the lawn of that house on August 17, 1940; my grandparents had married in Nantucket on that same date in 1918. At six or seven years old, I could be found standing at the end of the dock feeding the seagulls with a bag of Portuguese bread crusts or crawling around on the beach at low tide catching hermit crabs. There are so many highlights of those childhood summers, like swimming off their dock with my grandmother, Betty, who used to float down a house or two to see her friends Gilly and Willy Tolman. One summer afternoon, we children were titillated and horrified when we watched as they floated and chatted, and my grandmother swallowed a jellyfish. We would come in from swimming, race to change in the cabanas that ran along the side of the house, and then get ready to watch my grandfather play croquet with his cronies on the lawn. They would play into the night, laughing and sipping Southsider cocktails at the various wickets. Here is his famous brew.

SOUTHSIDERS

2 ounces Vodka
1/2 ounce Triple Sec
2 ounces fresh lime juice
2 ounces soda water
Fresh mint leaves

Mix first four ingredients and shake.

Pour over crushed ice.

Add mint leaves.

(For an even fresher taste, put first three ingredients in blender with mint leaves and chop. Add to glasses with ice and soda water.)

Carla

By the time I was 16, my father had bought a 42-foot yawl, which became our summer home. We had all been sailing all our lives, so we loved this. We would bring the boat to Nantucket Harbor and dock it at a berth for a month each summer. Because I was the oldest, I was often left in charge. I would have to make sure everyone did his or her appointed tasks, as well as cook dinner for the kids on the boat. Nothing fancy, but I did get inventive with my macaroni and cheese, which came to mean comfort in a new way.

In late August of that year, my parents had returned to Rhode Island to work, leaving me on the boat to watch over my younger sisters and brothers. A terrible storm hit. I felt pretty confident that we could ride it out well, and when you are 16 years old, you have no fears. My father had taught us how to fix the lines during inclement wind and weather conditions, so that was not the problem. It was the other boats. Several other sailboats moored out in the harbor kept coming alongside of us and asking to raft up to ride out the storm. Now, we really had not had that discussion with my Dad, but all I could think about was that we had enough to take care of ourselves without another sailing vessel pounding alongside us. Plus, there is always the risk of sailboats' rigging getting caught up in each other when the boats are rocking; this can pull a mast down in a flash, and someone can really get hurt. It was hard for me to say no to these people looking for some help, but I did, and my Dad was very happy that I made this decision. The wind howled, and we crashed around at our mooring for what seemed like a very long time. I was able to keep my siblings feeling safe and act like I knew what I was doing, but when it was over, I felt a relief that I can still remember. That night, when we were floating once again in calm waters, everyone was suddenly hungry, and I managed to make my first mac and cheese, which tasted mighty fabulous.

Here is the version I still make and often take to reheat at picnics:

Serves 8–10

Preheat oven to 350°

**1 pound of cooked elbow
  macaroni**
5 1/2 cups of milk
1/2 cup of flour
8 tablespoons butter
2 teaspoons salt
1/4 teaspoon nutmeg
1/4 teaspoon black pepper
1/4 teaspoon cayenne pepper
**4 1/2 cups grated sharp
  cheese**
2 cups grated Gruyère cheese
**1 green pepper, chopped
  (optional)**
**6 slices white bread,
  buttered and chopped**

Cook the macaroni according to package directions and set aside. Melt the butter. Add the flour, stirring to make a nice smooth sauce. Then, add the seasonings and cheeses and green pepper.

Cook for 1 minute, then toss with cooked macaroni. Pour mixture into 13" × 9" Pyrex dish. Then, sprinkle the buttered bread all over the top and bake uncovered for 45 minutes.

Sometimes I add a little grated onion too.

NANTUCKET MEMORIES

Carla

We always came here on my Dad's boat as kids and never wanted to leave. It was as though we never could get enough of the island. We looked forward to our Nantucket holiday all year, and it was the memories of the summer that got us through the winter. In late spring, we would start counting down the days until we would be setting sail for the island.

Now I do not leave very much. I live more on the island than any other place, and I really love it here, particularly through all the seasons, even in the dead of winter. It is sort of a hibernation time, and then, just when that begins to get old, the island starts to come alive again.

Over the years, I have lived in many different areas of the island and have found that each spot has its own charm. As for the endless debate, the truth is that it is fun to be in town; yet, it is also fun to be out in 'Sconset, which is a jewel. Nantucket Island is a treasured place, and I am happy to be anywhere on this rock and to have my many special friends.

When Debby and I first met on a beach, it was an instant friendship, and we have remained close friends through thick and thin. For many years, we both lived off island in the winter, in the places where our children attended school. Debby and I used to have an unannounced competition to see who could get back to Nantucket first. We would each arrive at our children's respective

schools on the final day of classes, with our cars fully loaded, and take off for the ferry. Our cars would be loaded with furniture and clothes, dogs and birds and children. Getting on the ferry, it would seem like we were going 3,000 miles away from America. Whoever's family arrived first was always there to greet the second family when their ferry pulled in. One year, after we had spent a long and sometimes lonely winter in England, I remember well the sight of Debby and her girls waving to us from the wharf. I can tear up now recalling how welcomed we felt and how happy we were to be back.

There was always such a wonderful sweet smell as we got off the ferry and drove to our house. No matter who won the race to get here, and I think it was usually me, we came to cherish those first weeks in June when it felt as though we had the island to ourselves. The fog seemed thicker, Main Street seemed empty, and we could negotiate our way through the supermarkets and hear our own footsteps on the cobblestones.

However, the best part of our summers here were our friendships, many of which were formed at beach picnics. I am happy that my children were able to have such wonderful experiences on this beautiful island, and I hope they will cherish those memories forever.

The recipes in this book have come to us from a myriad of sources, including family, friends, local chefs, and our own collections. We have attributed every known source, but if there is the odd recipe copied from a frayed saved newspaper column, or if a friend didn't remember where she got it, our apologies all around.

APPETIZERS

Asparagus and Ham Tarts 42

Autumn Bisque Soup 38

Barnacle Clam Chowder 39

Beet Soup.. 40

Blue Cheese and Caramelized Shallot Dip 30

Carla's Sand Dollars 43

Chili Con Queso... 33

Cream Cheese Crescents 44

Daisy's Dip.. 31

Figs with Blue Cheese and Prosciutto............................... 45

Grilled Sausage with Cheddar and Onions 46

Ham Rolls 47

Jerusalem Artichoke Soup 41

Nantucket Beach Bread... 48

Pineapple Curry.. 35

Shrimp Dip... 36

Smoky Babaganoush... 34

Smoked Bluefish Paté 49

Southwestern Pumpkin Seed Quesadillas.......................... 51

Sweet Coconut Dip.. 37

Warm Cheddar and Onion Dip....................................... 32

Serves 8

This is the hip contemporary version of the old favorite party dip. The blue cheese gives it sophistication and bite, and the shallots make you want to lick your fingers.

1 tablespoon vegetable oil
1 1/4 cups thinly sliced shallots
3/4 cup mayonnaise
3/4 cup sour cream
1/2 teaspoon dry mustard
1 teaspoon Worcestershire sauce
Salt and pepper to taste

Heat oil in heavy saucepan. Add shallots and cook until they are golden brown, stirring occasionally. Cool to room temperature.

Mix the mayonnaise, sour cream, dry mustard, and Worcestershire sauce together. Add the blue cheese and shallots.

This is great with all fresh summer vegetables, as well as chips.

Daisy and Steve Rapp have been beach picnic regulars over the last quarter-century. Daisy used to own and operate a children's clothing store called The Parrot on Main Street, and Steve is well known for his antique cars and trucks, which he drives in the Daffodil Day Parade. They love Nantucket and eagerly pitch in with the cooking and carrying at any picnics we arrange, and Daisy always brings this delicious dip.

4 ounce jar of pimento peppers
1 onion, minced
1 tablespoon Worcestershire sauce
8 ounces sharp cheddar cheese, shredded
4 tablespoons mayonnaise

Chop pimentos and combine all the ingredients in a bowl, including the juice from the jar of pimentos. Mix together with a fork, and add more mayonnaise if the mixture seems dry. Serve with Ritz crackers. This recipe can easily be doubled and stores well for several days.

Serves 6

This is another easy and scrumptious appetizer. It is important that you heat this at home shortly before leaving, wrap it tightly in foil, and set it out warm on the picnic table. Our choice of cracker is Wheat Thins; however, you will also find it delicious on a chip or pita bread. It, too, has become a regular feature of our picnics.

Preheat oven to 400°

1 onion, minced
8 ounces shredded cheddar cheese
1 cup light mayonnaise

Combine all ingredients and put in an ovenproof dish. Bake for 30 minutes or until brown and bubbling.

Serves a crowd

Gooey, spicy, Tex-Mex all the way, this is one you make at home and heat up when you get your grill fire lit. We have probably served this at every big party we have ever had, and not one time was there a remnant left in the pot. (When you serve it at home and don't have the advantage of a warm fire, it works best in a chafing dish.) For easier clean up, bring a nonstick skillet to the party or a cast-iron pan, and bring the contents already warmed up so that you can make it available more quickly. This recipe is for a crowd, so bring plenty of tortilla chips.

1 pound bacon
2 onions, chopped
2 jalapeno peppers, seeded and chopped (optional)
1 can peeled, drained tomatoes
8 ounces canned diced green chilies
1 pound grated sharp cheddar cheese
1 teaspoon cumin powder
1 teaspoon chili powder
Tortilla chips

Cook bacon, drain and crumble. Set aside. Pour off grease and cook onion in coated pan. Add jalapenos and cook with onion. Add tomatoes and chilies and return bacon to pan. Add cheese and seasonings to taste. Melt cheese and serve with tortilla chips.

Serves 8

It is always a bonus to have summer vegetables available. Eggplants are stacked up at the farmer's market, and they make a great grilled vegetable at a picnic. They also make a marvelous dip. The smoky flavor of the grill enhances this babaganoush, and it is quickly assembled once the eggplants have cooled down.

2 eggplants, halved
1/2 cup lemon juice
2 cloves garlic, chopped
1/4 cup olive oil
Salt and pepper

Score each eggplant half. Salt the pieces and turn them over a strainer for about 20 minutes to release moisture. Take to beach, brush with oil, and set on outside part of grill where coals are less intense. Grill flesh side down first for about 10 minutes, then flip. Cook until flesh is softened.

Set the grilled eggplant aside until cool enough to handle. Using a fork, mash the eggplant into a bowl, adding the lemon and olive oil until it is smooth. Add chopped garlic and seasonings. Serve with celery sticks, bread, or crackers.

Serves 6–8

Carla

While we were living in England, a gal who was definitely another Martha, Cindi Reid, made this for one of our parties and was very kind to share the recipe with some of her ex-pat friends in the neighborhood. The presentation is lovely, and the flavors are sensational. This makes a great opener to any beach picnic party and pairs well with a light sauvignon blanc.

8 ounces cream cheese, softened
1/4 cup chutney (any kind will do)
1/4 teaspoon dry mustard
1 teaspoon curry powder
1 fresh pineapple
Almonds, toasted
Crackers of your choice

Mix cream cheese, chutney, dry mustard, and curry thoroughly. Chill for 4 hours. (It is very important to make the mixture ahead of time to get the best flavor.)

Cut the pineapple in half from top to bottom, but do not cut off the leaves. Hollow out and save the pineapple chunks for a salad or a dessert. When ready to serve, fill the pineapple with the cream cheese mixture and top with the toasted almonds. Serve with the crackers of your choice.

Makes 6 cups

The original recipe calls for cooking your own shrimp, but we find it much easier to buy the shrimp already prepared for shrimp cocktail, particularly if you are running out of time. It is also better to chill the dip for a few hours before serving so all the flavors come forth.

2 1/2 pounds medium-sized shrimp
1/2 green pepper, quartered
1/2 onion, quartered
2 sticks celery, cut in pieces
1 garlic clove, peeled
11 ounces cream cheese, softened
3 tablespoon mayonnaise
2 tablespoon lemon juice
1/2 teaspoon salt
1/4 teaspoon cayenne pepper

Set aside two of the shrimp for garnish and pulse the rest in the food processor 4–5 times or until chopped. Set aside. Pulse the bell pepper, onion, celery, and garlic until chopped and add to the shrimp. Process the cream cheese and next four ingredients until fluffy. Add to the shrimp mixture and chill for several hours. Before serving, garnish with two shrimps.

Serves 20

This dip is at its best during the summer months when the fruits are at their ripest. We have often made it when we have gone strawberry picking with friends and gone overboard with the number of berries we have picked.
This dip works well with a light glass of white wine.

8 ounces of cream cheese, softened
8 ounces of sour cream
1/2 cup of cream of coconut
1 cup macaroons, crumbled
2 tablespoons brown sugar
1 teaspoon cinnamon
1/2 teaspoon nutmeg
1/2 teaspoon ginger
Dash of lemon juice

Mix all of the ingredients together in a medium-sized mixing bowl and chill overnight or at least for 4 hours. Serve with strawberries, melons, kiwis, apples, bananas, or any other fruit you like.

Serves 6

This recipe came out of a newspaper about 20 years ago and has traveled everywhere with us. We can barely read it now, but it has been enjoyed by many people around the world. The original recipe called for adding heavy cream to the soup just before serving. However, we have never felt that it needed this addition, as it is a smooth, rich-tasting soup as it is. It is perfect for a fall beach picnic and will definitely warm you up on a cool, crisp day.

1 pound butternut squash, pared, halved, seeded, and cubed
2 tart apples, pared, cored, and cubed
1 onion, chopped
2 slices white bread, trimmed and cubed
4 cups chicken broth
1 1/2 teaspoon salt
1/4 teaspoon pepper
1/4 teaspoon ground rosemary
1/4 teaspoon ground marjoram

Combine the squash, apples, onion, bread, chicken broth, salt, pepper, rosemary, and marjoram in a large saucepan. Bring to a boil. Lower heat and simmer uncovered for 35 minutes or until the squash and apples are tender. Remove from heat and cool to lukewarm.

Working in batches, spoon the soup into the container of the food processor. Cover and pulse until pureed. Return the soup to the saucepan and reheat gently over low heat.

Serves 8

Ruth Barney married into an old Nantucket family and waded right into every Nantucket pastime, including clamming, which she does with alacrity. She lives with her family in the Barnacle, one of the last original wharf cottages, whose sloping sides and roof give it a fairy-tale quality. When she can tear herself from her waterside deck, she brings her fabulous clam chowder to begin our beach picnics, and there is never a drop to lug home. This is her utterly fresh, totally traditional, coveted recipe. This recipe tastes better the second day, so you can feel comfortable making it ahead of time.

3 - 4 onions, chopped
1/2 pound bacon (cut in pieces)
8 red potatoes with skins on
1 cup water
1 quart of clams,
**   chopped with their broth**
1–2 pints heavy whipping cream

Sauté the onions and bacon in a chowder pot until onion is transparent. Then, chop up red potatoes into cubes and add to onion and bacon. Cook for 10 minutes, stirring so the mixture does not stick to the pan. Add 1 cup of water, cover, and simmer to steam potatoes. Once potatoes are cooked, add the clams and broth, then turn off the heat, and let everything sit. It's great to make this base in the morning and finish it up at dinnertime.

When almost ready to serve, add 1–2 pints of heavy cream and heat slowly so that it does not boil.

Serves 4

This soup is such a beautiful shade of magenta that the color alone would make it a welcome addition to your picnic table. But as pretty as it is, the taste is even better—cool, sweet, savory, and simple. Make it ahead of time, chill it, and serve it with snipped fresh chives or dill. It is a quick and easy lunch, and a great appetizer while you are waiting for the grill to heat up.

Preheat oven to 450°

1 bunch of beets
1 teaspoon butter
1/2 cup red onion
8 cups chicken broth
Salt and pepper
1 pint light or heavy cream, sour cream, or yogurt

Cut stems off beets and wrap them in tin foil. Reserve stems for other use. Roast the beets for 1 hour and rinse under cold water, slipping off the skins. Roughly chop beets and put in blender. Sauté onion in butter until soft and add to blender. Pour in chicken stock. Purée and season to taste. Add your choice of thickener and blend again.

Serves 4

Jerusalem artichokes—also called sunchokes—are a great find in your supermarket aisle. They look like ginger root and taste sweet and crunchy when raw. We love to cook them in olive oil and garlic as they pick up all of the flavor, but for a picnic, they add a surprisingly interesting taste to a summer soup.

Like most soups, this one works cool or warm. Peel the chokes, but don't worry if a little skin gets in. They are knobby little items, so just sacrifice a few bumps for efficiency. Once you sample them, you will find plenty of ways to use them in lieu of potatoes as a gratin or side dish, or in this lovely soup.

1 pound Jerusalem artichokes, scrubbed and peeled
1 tablespoon butter
1 tablespoon oil
1 1/2 cups onion, chopped
4 cups chicken broth
1 teaspoon fresh lemon juice
1 cup heavy cream
Chopped chives
Salt and pepper

Peel the sunchokes and boil until you can pierce them with a fork, then drain. Heat oil and butter and sauté onion until soft. Put onion and drained chokes in blender and add lemon juice, broth, and heavy cream. Blend in batches and season to taste. Serve warm or cool with chopped fresh chives.

Serves 18

This is a great appetizer to make for a beach picnic, as the tarts are delicious served warm or cold. We use mini muffin tins; however, if you want to serve them for a luncheon, you can make them in regular-sized muffin tins.

Preheat oven to 425°

1/4 cup butter, softened
1 3-ounce package cream cheese, softened
3/4 cup flour
1/4 cup yellow cornmeal
2 tablespoons Dijon mustard
3/4 cup Swiss cheese, shredded
1 tablespoon flour
1 egg
1/3 cup light cream
1/2 cup diced ham
18 1-inch asparagus tips

Mix the cream cheese and butter together, and stir in the 3/4 cup flour and the cornmeal. Cover and chill for 1 hour. Shape the dough into 18 balls, approximately 1-inch in size. Place the balls in miniature muffin tins and press evenly into the bottom and sides. Spread a little of the mustard on the bottom of each pastry shell. Stir together the Swiss cheese and the tablespoon of flour. Whisk together the egg and light cream, then stir the Swiss cheese mixture and the ham into the pastry shells.

Bake for 7 minutes, then top each tart with an asparagus spear. Reduce the oven heat to 300° and bake for 20 minutes more.

Makes approximately 2 dozen

People always seem to enjoy this appetizer, and even though we worry that they will tire of it, there is never a sand dollar left on the plate. We keep the dough in the freezer, so they are always only minutes away.

Preheat oven to 375°

4 tablespoons butter, softened
1 cup jalapeno cheddar cheese, shredded
1/2 cup sifted flour
1/4 teaspoon salt
Cayenne pepper (to taste)
1/4 teaspoon dry mustard
Poppy or sesame seeds

Mix first six ingredients in medium-sized bowl. Roll into a log, wrap in wax paper, and refrigerate overnight. Slice 1/4 inch thick and place on an ungreased cookie sheet. With a toothpick, make indentations that replicate a sand dollar and fill with the poppy seeds. Bake for 10 minutes. The logs may be made up and kept in the refrigerator for up to a week or kept frozen.

CREAM CHEESE CRESCENTS

Makes 3 dozen

This appetizer recipe seems to please everyone's taste buds, and it has traveled with me for many years, even back and forth to England. It is a sweet appetizer, and especially appreciated by the little ones at a beach picnic. We bake this at home and take it to the beach in a Styrofoam cooler to keep if hot.

Preheat oven to 350°

36 slices white bread
1 container of whipped cream cheese
2 sticks margarine or butter
Cinnamon, nutmeg, and granulated sugar

Remove crusts from bread slices and roll thin with rolling pin. Cut each piece of bread in half and spread with cream cheese and roll up. Dip in melted butter or margarine, roll in sugar mixture, shape into crescent and place on cookie sheet. When you have filled the sheet, stick in the freezer for several hours. When they are frozen, you may store them in a Ziploc bag. When you are ready to serve take the crescents directly from the freezer, place on an ungreased cookie sheet and bake for 15 to 20 minutes or until brown.

This appetizer stores well in the freezer for weeks.

Serves 8

With so much produce being shipping around the world, it seems like we can get almost anything all the time. Fresh figs, however, are one of few fruits that only appear in season. For that reason, they maintain their value as a treat, and we delight at their appearance on the supermarket produce shelf. Figs are great in desserts, poached in syrup and served with ice cream, but they also make a great hors d'oeuvres. These are quick to assemble and grill up in minutes.

24 figs, split
8 ounces creamy blue cheese, like Roquefort or Cashel blue
1/4 pound sliced prosciutto
Toothpicks, soaked in water

Put a dollop of blue cheese inside each fig. Wrap with a slice of prosciutto and secure with a damp toothpick. Place on grill and cook until cheese is melted. Use tongs to turn and remove.

Serves a crowd

When we have an especially large gathering and everyone needs to have a bite while waiting, this appetizer is just the ticket. One summer FedEx pilot Oliver Coolidge and his California-blonde wife, Jill, joined us, and she brought these ingredients along. Since then, they are a regular feature at our picnics. Great Italian sausage, either sweet or hot, is especially delicious on the grill. A crusty baguette, some sharp cheddar, and a slice of red onion make for a satisfying treat. Assemble as you hand them out.

1 pound Italian sausage, sweet or hot
1 brick extra sharp cheddar cheese
1 red onion
Dijon mustard
Crusty rolls

Grill sausage, cut into 2-inch slices, and split down middle. Split open rolls and spread with mustard. Slice onions and cheddar. When sausage is cooked, place in roll with onions and cheddar and serve as a warm sandwich.

Serves 6

This is an easy picnic appetizer that would work just as well as an entrée served with a green salad. We like to put the ham and cheese mixture into petite rolls for appetizers, and big crusty French rolls for dinner. They are especially welcome on a cool evening. Either way, they should be wrapped in foil and heated on the grill until the cheese is warm and runny.

6 hard petite rolls or French rolls
1 pound of ham, ground
1/4 pound jalapeno cheddar cheese, grated
1/2 pound Swiss cheese, grated
8-10 green olives, chopped
6 green onions, chopped
2 celery stalks, chopped
1/2 cup olive oil
1/2 cup tomato paste

Scrape out and butter the center of the rolls. Mix all the other ingredients together in a food processor and fill the rolls. Wrap well with foil. Put on the grill for 10 to 15 minutes until the cheese has melted.

Serves 8

This is a delicious take on hot herbed bread—hearty, cheesy, filling, and packed with flavor.

Preheat oven to 350°

1/4 pound plus 2 tablespoons butter
2 teaspoons Dijon mustard
1 onion, finely chopped
2 tablespoons poppy seeds
2 tablespoons lemon juice
8 ounces Monterey Jack cheese, sliced
1 loaf French bread

Combine the first five ingredients in a saucepan and simmer until onions are soft. Slice bread diagonally about 1 inch thick. Do not cut through the bottom crust. Spread butter mixture in between slices. Stuff each cut with cheese. Wrap in foil, leaving part of the top exposed. Bake in oven or on top of grill for 20 minutes.

Bluefish are as common to Nantucket as hydrangeas and roses. The fishermen may wait an hour or so for the bluefish to run by, but when they do, they chop up the water and swim in huge schools, and suddenly they are reeled in by the numbers. Therefore, there is a constant need to find innovative ways to use up that bluefish, and this paté which comes from 'Sconseter Barbara Nowak, is a big favorite. She is a great cook and an eager beach picnicker who always shows up with a memorable dish.

Preheat oven to 350°

8 ounces smoked bluefish,
   shredded
1 package cream cheese
   (not light)
1 tablespoon horseradish
1 chopped shallot
2 tablespoons mayonnaise
2 teaspoons Worcestershire sauce
Tabasco sauce
Fresh lemon juice
Salt and pepper to taste

Blend all ingredients in a food processor to the consistency desired. Crab meat may be used in place of the bluefish. If a hot spread is desired, bake in a greased gratin dish for approximately 30 minutes.

Garnish with toasted slivered almonds or capers.

49

Serves 10

Deborah

About 20 years ago, Sarah Leah Chase operated her own gourmet shop called Que Sera Sarah. Even though the shop is long gone, many of us remember lining up for the tempting dishes arranged in her cases. Once her *Open House Cookbook* came out, we busily duplicated her great recipes. Sarah, a Harvard graduate and a fabulous writer, put all her intelligence and energy into cooking and teaching. She taught at RISD when I ran the Culinary School there, and she came to Cooks and Books. This recipe comes from one of those classes Sarah taught years ago. I offer it with belated thanks to Sarah.

Preheat oven to 350°

2 cups hulled, unsalted pumpkin seeds
1/3 cup olive oil (separate out 2 tablespoons)
1 jalapeno pepper, seeded and minced
2 cloves garlic, minced
1/3 cup fresh lime juice
1 cup fresh chicken broth
1/2 teaspoon ground cumin
1/4 teaspoon salt
1/3 cup fresh cilantro
2–3 cups Monterey Jack cheese, shredded

Toast pumpkin seeds for 10 minutes. Cool slightly. Heat two tablespoons of olive oil over medium-high heat. Add jalapeno and garlic, and cook until softened, about 2 minutes. Place pumpkin seeds, sautéed jalapeno and garlic, and lime juice in food processor fitted with steel blade. Process to form thick paste. With machine running, add remaining olive oil and enough chicken broth to make a smooth dip. Season with cumin and salt. Add cilantro. Pulse until chopped.

Spread an 8-inch flour tortilla with a generous coating of the pumpkin seed dip, then sprinkle generously with shredded jack cheese. Top with another flour tortilla.

Make as many quesadillas as desired. Arrange on a baking sheet and bake until slightly crisp and the cheese is melted. Keep warm in foil. When ready to serve, cut into wedges. If taking these to the beach, let the foil-enclosed quesadillas warm over the grills for several minutes before cutting and serving.

Asian Cole Slaw 57

Balsamic Risotto Salad 55

Chickpea Salad 56

Cold Chinese Noodles 58

French Potato Salad with Fines Herbes 60

Fruit Salad with Lime Marinade 59

Green Bean and Basil Salad 61

Green Salad with Avocado And Citrus Dressing 62

Orange Poppyseed Salad 63

Spinach Salad with Apricot Vinaigrette 64

Summer Beet Salad 66

Thai Cucumber Salad 65

Ultimate Corn Salad 67

Watermelon Salad 69

White Bean Salad 70

Serves 10

We first had a version of this dish at the amazing Italian market Venda Ravioli in Providence, Rhode Island. The chef gave us a recipe, which we have adapted here. This is a great dish for a crowd, with a wonderful texture and taste, and it keeps for a week in the refrigerator should you have any left over.

3 cups Arborio rice
6 cups water
2 cups portobello mushroom caps
1 cup sliced roasted red peppers
12 ounces fresh baby spinach
1/2 cup balsamic vinegar
6 cloves chopped garlic
1 cup olive oil
Salt and pepper

Add rice to boiling water and cook for about 30 minutes. It will not be fully cooked but will finish cooking in the dressing. Drain rice under cold water and put in bowl. Slice portobello mushrooms and add to rice. Add sliced roasted red peppers and fresh spinach. Add vinegar. Heat oil, and add garlic. Brown lightly and pour hot oil over spinach. Let stand for a couple of minutes and then toss the rice to distribute the spinach and peppers and mushrooms. Add salt and pepper and season to taste. Serve at room temperature.

Serves 4–6

Chickpeas are one of those staples we always have in the pantry. They are delicious tossed in oil and garlic salt and toasted in the oven, where they become a nutty satisfying snack food. As a salad, they work beautifully, soaking up the flavors of the dressing but retaining a crunchy texture. This salad is beautiful to look at and better to eat.

2 cans chickpeas, drained and rinsed
1 red onion, chopped
1 red pepper, chopped
1 green pepper, chopped
2 cloves garlic, minced
1/2 cup olive oil
1/3 cup balsamic vinegar
1/2 bunch basil, chopped
Salt and pepper

Combine first five ingredients and toss to mix. Add dressing and basil, and season to taste. If you prefer cilantro or another herb to basil, it will only compliment this crunchy and healthy salad.

Serves 8

Deborah

This recipe has been passed around the country for years in various presentations, and this version originated with my Canadian sister-in-law. We take it to every picnic because it is easy and feeds many people. My preference is to go heavy on the rice vinegar, which is the essential ingredient in the salad. I use the Marukan brand, which eliminates the need for sugar. Light and filling, it is a guiltless treat that stretches many a meal. I like to dress the slaw shortly before serving because I love the crisp texture. The cabbage does absorb the dressing and soften up very quickly, though it is good in any case.

1 head green cabbage, shredded
1 bunch scallions, chopped, including green parts
1/2 cup slivered almonds
1 package Ramen noodles
1 bunch of cilantro, chopped
1/2 cup vegetable oil
1/2 cup rice vinegar
Salt and pepper

Put cabbage and scallions into a bowl and toss. Pour vegetable oil into a skillet, and lightly brown the almonds. Remove almonds with slotted spoon and add to the slaw. Turn off heat and add the rice vinegar. (It will spatter slightly.)

Pour dressing onto slaw mix. Crumble dried ramen noodles and add to slaw. Add cilantro. Toss again, and salt and pepper to taste.

Serves 6–8

There was one summer when we were never without Sarah Chase's Cold Chinese Noodles, a dish that is easy to make and seems to appeal to young and old alike. We are offering our version of that salad for those who never had a chance to eat at Sarah's lovely shop or read her wonderful cookbook.

5 ounces ham, julienned
1 bunch scallions, chopped, including green parts
1/2 cup chopped walnuts
1 pound vermicelli, cooked al dente and rinsed
**   under cold water**
3/4 cup vegetable oil
2 tablespoons sesame oil
3 teaspoons sesame seeds
3 tablespoons ground coriander seeds
3/4 cup soy sauce
1 teaspoon (or to taste) hot chili oil

Mix first three ingredients together, and combine with cooked pasta. In a sauté pan, heat the oil and gently toast the sesame seeds. Add the soy sauce and the coriander, and be careful of the spatter. Pour hot dressing over noodles and toss well, preferably with your hands. Add chili oil to taste.

Serves 10–12

Nothing tastes more refreshing at a beach picnic than a bowl of fresh fruit, and it seems that we always have this on our menu for our get-togethers. The limeade in this recipe is the secret ingredient that adds a nice flavor.

1/2 seedless watermelon
1 cantaloupe
1 pint strawberries
2 kiwis
1 pint blueberries
3/4 pound seedless red or green grapes
1/3 cup frozen limeade concentrate, thawed

Cut the melons into small pieces and slice the strawberries and peeled kiwi. Combine all the fruit in a large bowl and stir in the limeade.

Serves 10

This potato salad is far superior, in our minds, to mayonnaise-based potato salads. It is savory and exceedingly fresh. Do not substitute dried herbs, as it is the delicate taste of the fresh herbs that makes this dish sing. Naturally, you can vary the dressing ingredients to your taste, increasing the mustard or vinegar. We love the sharp taste of both those ingredients, so we always add more. The same is true for the wine. The wine gives this dish its distinction, and after you have made it once, you may want to add a whole cup of white wine, instead of half. In any case, since this potato salad does not use mayonnaise, the salad can keep at room temperature for a long time. If you have leftovers, fry them up in a skillet the next day as a tasty garlicky side dish for dinner.

4 pounds red-skinned potatoes
1/2 cup white wine

Dressing
1 cup extra virgin olive oil
1/2 cup red wine vinegar
1/2 cup Dijon mustard, preferably Maille
1 bunch chives, finely chopped
3 cloves garlic, minced
6 sprigs fresh thyme, leaves only, chopped
1/4 cup fresh parsley, finely chopped
1/2 cup fresh rosemary, finely chopped
Salt and pepper to taste

Quarter the potatoes and boil gently until you can pierce with a fork (about 12 minutes). While the potatoes are cooking, prepare the dressing. Drain the potatoes, put in a bowl, and pour wine over them. (Once you have made this recipe, you may want to add more wine because it enriches the flavor, but not more than 1 cup.) Let sit for 2 minutes, and add the dressing while the potatoes are still warm. Stir to insure all the potatoes are dressed. Season with salt and pepper. Cover and serve at room temperature.

Serves 4

This is a lovely summer alternative to a lettuce salad. There is a great deal of flavor with the different textures and fresh tastes. It is also colorful and healthy. This adds a lot to a simple grilled fish or chicken as it packs the flavor and compliments grilled food. As the dressing continues to be absorbed, beans pick up flavor, meaning it will make a great leftover as well.

1 pound green beans, blanched in salted water
1 ripe summer tomato, chopped
1 shallot, finely chopped
1/2 bunch fresh basil, julienned
1/3 cup chopped black olives

Vinaigrette
1/2 cup olive oil
1/3 cup balsamic vinegar
1 clove garlic, minced
1 teaspoon Dijon mustard
Salt and pepper

Cook the beans to your taste. Drain and cool. Chop tomato, and salt liberally. Chop shallot and basil. Toss beans in vinaigrette with shallot and basil. Arrange on plate, and top with drained chopped tomatoes and olives.

Serves 6

This salad is not only full of color but totally refreshing. The citrus dressing makes all the difference here. It is a great side dish, but if you want to make a meal out of it, add grilled chicken or steak. Assemble all the ingredients into your serving bowl at home and toss the salad at the beach.

2 heads of romaine
3 ripe plum tomatoes, sliced
2 ripe avocados
1 onion, sliced
1 cup crumbled Gorgonzola cheese

Dressing
1 cup olive oil
1/3 cup grapefruit juice
1/3 cup orange juice
1 tablespoon zest from orange and grapefruit
1 clove garlic, chopped
Salt and pepper

Wash romaine and break it into small bite-sized pieces. Slice avocado and chop into 1-inch cubes. Slice onion and soak in water to remove sharp taste. (Take onion out after half an hour with three water changes.) Add onion and tomatoes to lettuce, and add crumbled cheese. Toss with dressing and serve.

Serves 6

Carla

This salad has been created from the original mandarin orange salad that my friend Stephanie shared with me while we were ex-pats in England. The caramelized almonds give it crunch and a boost of flavor. I have served it at bridal luncheons and at many dinner parties, where I notice that the men seem to enjoy it just as much as the ladies.

1/2 cup sliced almonds
2 tablespoons sugar
1 head Boston lettuce
1 head leaf lettuce
20 fresh strawberries, sliced
1 11-ounce can mandarin oranges, drained
1 green onion, chopped
2 stalks celery, chopped
3/4 cup olive oil
1/4 cup red wine vinegar
1 teaspoon grated orange rind
1 tablespoon fresh orange juice
1 teaspoon poppy seeds
Salt and pepper to taste

Caramelize the almonds by putting the sugar and almonds in a skillet (I use my electric pan) and heating over low heat until all the almonds are glazed. Put the almonds on a piece of wax paper to cool.

Toss together the lettuces with the strawberries, mandarin oranges, onion, and celery. Whisk together the olive oil with the next six ingredients. Pour the dressing on the salad, and add the caramelized almonds.

Serves 6

One summer we made this salad for practically every party that we either gave or went to, and it was enjoyed by everyone. We believe it is the apricot flavor in the vinaigrette that makes the salad notable.

1/3 cup olive oil
2 tablespoons red wine vinegar
2 tablespoons orange juice
2 tablespoons apricot jam
1/4 teaspoon salt
1/2 teaspoon freshly ground pepper
1/4 teaspoon ground coriander
1 package baby spinach
1 pint grape tomatoes
1/2 red onion, sliced thin
3/4 cup dried apricots, chopped
1/2 cup goat cheese, crumbled
1 avocado, peeled and diced
1/2 cup chopped pecans (optional)

Whisk together the first five ingredients and set aside. Mix the baby spinach together with the next six ingredients and then drizzle the apricot vinaigrette over the salad.

Serves 4

Always refreshing, cucumbers provide a counterpoint to grilled hamburgers or sweet and sour chicken dishes like Chicken Gai Yang or the Sticky Chicky. This salad comes together in a couple of minutes and offers crunch, sweetness, and the clean, acid taste of vinegar.

4 cucumbers, peeled and sliced thinly
2 red onions, peeled and minced
1/2 cup light corn syrup
3 tablespoons white vinegar
1 teaspoon salt
1 tablespoon sweet chili sauce

Add onions to sliced cucumbers. Mix next four ingredients together, and dress cucumbers.

Serves 8

Even folks wary of beets succumb to this salad. We made it recently for a wedding party dinner. The hostess was basically being polite by letting us put beets on the menu, but in the end, there wasn't a beet left on the table, and the hostess asked for the recipe. This is a great way to add color to your dinner, and since you are roasting the beets, they are easy to peel, and you are keeping in all the nutrition. This dish is quick to prepare and great the next day. We guarantee it will become one of your summer staples.

Preheat oven to 400°

2 bunches of beets
1/2 cup olive oil
1/2 cup balsamic vinegar
1/4 cup Dijon mustard
6 scallions, chopped, including green parts
2/3 cup walnuts, crushed
1/2 pound Roquefort cheese, crumbled
Salt and pepper

Cut beets off stems. Wash and reserve beet greens. Wrap unpeeled beets in tin foil and roast for 1 hour. Cool and rinse beets under cold water. The skins will slip off easily in your fingers. Slice beets. Combine dressing ingredients, and toss beets in the dressing. Add scallions, walnuts, and cheese. Season with salt and pepper. Line a bowl with the beet greens and put the salad in the middle. Serve at room temperature.

Serves 10

Corn salad is always a crowd pleaser. The avocado takes it from delicious to sublime, and the seasonings can be adjusted to the crowd's preference. We like it packed with punch, so we go heavy on the spices.

Note: We hate to give this dish up when the corn season ends, so we prepare it with 4 cans of drained shoepeg corn, a worthy substitute.

12 ears fresh corn off the cob
2 cans black beans, drained and rinsed
1 red onion, chopped
1 red pepper, chopped
1 green pepper, chopped
1 jalapeno, chopped
1 ripe tomato, seeded and chopped
2 avocados, chopped
1 bunch cilantro, chopped

Dressing
1/2 cup vegetable oil
1/3 cup fresh lime juice
1 tablespoon ground cumin
1 tablespoon chili powder
Salt and pepper

Combine the first nine ingredients, and stir to distribute. Pour dressing over salad, and season to taste: if you prefer it hotter, add more jalapeno or spiced red pepper flakes; if you like it tarter, add more lime juice. The cumin and chili powder can be added to suit your palate.

Serves 6–8

This is an unusual salad, that combines fruits and vegetables that you don't ordinarily see together. What you end up with is a colorful, fresh, textured, interesting, and completely delicious summer salad. It compliments the egg dishes we have in our brunch section or a quiche. The watermelon is so sweet and cool that this becomes a very refreshing dish, particularly on a hot day.

4 cups seedless watermelon, cubed
2 cups cherry tomatoes, halved
1/2 cup feta cheese, crumbled
2 cups spring lettuces
1 cup watercress, stems removed
2 tablespoons olive oil
2 tablespoons balsamic vinegar
1 tablespoon honey
Salt and pepper to taste
1/4 cup fresh mint, chopped

Place lettuces and watercress on a large serving platter or in a serving bowl. Place watermelon, tomatoes, and cheese on the greens. Mix together the olive oil, vinegar, honey, salt, and pepper. Drizzle over salad, and add the fresh mint on top.

Serves 4

White beans soak up the flavor around them, and they make a lovely alternative to potatoes or pasta as a side dish. This ultrasimple salad is healthy, filling, and savory. If you want to make this a meal, you might add tuna or Italian sausage.

2 cans white cannellini beans, drained and rinsed
1 large tomato, seeded and chopped
1 red onion, chopped

Dressing
1/2 cup extra virgin olive oil
1/3 cup fresh lemon juice or white wine vinegar
1 garlic clove, minced
Salt and pepper
Chopped fresh basil or parsley

Mix first three ingredients together. Add dressing and toss. Add herbs at serving time for maximum freshness.

Berry Streusel French Toast 74

Brant Point Brunch 75

Chicken Salad Sandwiches with Olive Paste 82

Clotted Cream 78

Crabmeat and Egg Lasagna 76

Cream Cheese and Date Sandwiches 81

Cucumber Tea Sandwiches 83

Egg Salad Tea Sandwiches 84

Hearty Egg and Bacon Brunch 79

Island Tea Sandwiches 85

Rosemary Chicken Salad Tea Sandwiches 86

True English Scones 77

Watercress and Stilton Tea Sandwiches 80

Serves 6–8

Our friend Ruth Barney made this delicious brunch dish one Sunday morning. It must be prepared the night before so that the bread soaks up the egg mixture, and then it is popped in the oven the morning it is served. We've brought this treat to our picnics. Nothing is better than sipping coffee on a beautiful morning on a pretty beach in Nantucket and then indulging in this wonderful brunch dish. You bake it at home, then wrap it well in foil, and it travels very well to the beach. You can also transport it to the beach in a cooler to keep it extra hot.

Preheat oven to 375°

1 loaf sliced Italian bread
6 eggs
4 tablespoons granulated sugar
2 1/4 cups milk
1 teaspoon vanilla
2 cups blueberries, raspberries, strawberries
  (any combination will do)
1/4 cup margarine or butter
1/2 cup flour
1/2 cup brown sugar
Sifted powdered sugar
Maple syrup

The night before, beat together the eggs, sugar, vanilla, and milk. Put the bread slices in a greased 9" x 13" pan, making sure to cover as much of the bottom of the pan as possible (cutting smaller pieces to fit in open spaces). Spread egg mixture over bread, cover, and refrigerate overnight.

Next morning, sprinkle the fruit over the bread mixture. Combine the margarine or butter with the flour and brown sugar until it is crumbly, then sprinkle over the top of the fruit and bake for 35–40 minutes until puffy and set. Cut into serving pieces, sprinkle with sifted powdered sugar, and serve with maple syrup.

Serves 8

Take this egg and bacon casserole down to the Brant Point Beach on a Sunday morning and watch the ferries come and go as you indulge in this dish. It is also perfect for a supper picnic as well.

Preheat oven to 300°

1 10-ounce package of frozen hash browns
4 tablespoons butter
1/2 cup chopped onions
1/4 cup flour
1/2 teaspoon salt
1/8 teaspoon freshly ground pepper
2 cups milk
1 cup sour cream
2 tablespoons parsley, chopped
8 slices Canadian bacon
8 eggs
Salt and pepper

Prepare the hash browns according to the package directions. Melt the butter in a saucepan and sauté the onion. Add the flour, salt, and pepper and blend. Add the milk all at once and cook, stirring until thick and bubbling. Remove from the heat and add sour cream, parsley, and hash browns. Put in a 13" x 9" buttered casserole dish. Arrange the bacon on top and bake for 20 minutes. Remove from oven, make eight depressions with a spoon, and place eggs in them. Bake for 20 minutes more, or until the eggs are set.

Serves 8

This is one of our favorite recipes because we can make it ahead of time and just pop it in the oven when we are ready, or we can even take it to the beach and wrap it in foil and cook it on the grill. It's quick to put together and goes nicely with a flank steak, making it a surf-and-turf kind of brunch.

Preheat oven to 350°

1 pound bacon
1/2 cup onion, chopped
1/3 cup flour
1/2 teaspoon salt
1/2 teaspoon freshly ground pepper
4 cups milk
12 lasagna noodles, cooked
3 6-ounce cans crabmeat, drained and flaked
12 eggs, hard-boiled and sliced
8 ounces cheddar cheese, grated

Cook bacon until crisp. Drain on a paper towel and cut into small pieces. Sauté onions in a little bit of the bacon drippings. Then, add the flour, salt, and pepper and cook over medium heat until smooth. Then, add the milk and cook until thickened, stirring constantly. Grease a 13" x 9" pan and layer with some of the sauce, noodles, bacon, crabmeat, remaining sauce, eggs, and cheese. Bake for 30 minutes.

Serves 6

Carla

Several years ago, my friend Peter Greenhalgh and I gave a tea party together at his home in ' Sconset. I watched in amazement as Peter whipped up these fabulous scones that his friend, Julie Wilson, had taught him how to make. She had lived for some time with an English family and come back to the U.S. with this truly English recipe. It really works, despite the untraditional way of measuring.

Preheat oven to 350°

3 teacupfuls flour
2 level cereal spoons baking powder
1/4 pound fat (butter)
1/2 teacupful sugar
6 big spoonfuls milk
Raisins (if desired)
Extra milk

Mix together the flour and baking powder, then rub in the softened fat. Add the sugar and raisins (if desired) and then add the milk and mix all together. Roll the dough out to 1/2-inch thickness and cut into 2–3-inch rounds. Brush a little milk on the top and bake for 15–20 minutes.

Serves 8–10

Carla

A scone is not very good unless you have jam and clotted cream. In the summertime, we love to pick our own strawberries and make jam. Nothing tastes better than a nice fresh scone with homemade jam and clotted cream! However, when I moved back to the States, I could not find clotted cream in any of the stores, but then I was so lucky that an English friend shared the ingredients in clotted cream with me, and I was able to make my own. It surely tastes like the real thing.

1/3 cup sour cream
1 cup heavy whipping cream
2 tablespoons powdered sugar

Pour the whipping cream into a large bowl and beat with an electric mixer until soft peaks form. Then, add the sour cream and sugar, and beat until it is all mixed and thick. Store in the refrigerator until ready to use.

Serves 6–8

When you need something a little more substantial on your brunch menu, this dish will provide it. Combining the ham, sausage, and bacon gives it a rich, hearty texture. This recipe is easy to throw together and filling, and it uses the time-honored flavor hit of cheese and eggs. It is a staple and always popular with the menfolk.

Preheat oven to 325°

4 slices white bread, cubed
6 eggs, beaten
3/4 cup milk
1/2 cup cooked ham, diced
1/2 cup smoked sausage, diced
1/2 cup bacon, crumbled
1/2 cup Swiss cheese, shredded
1/2 cup cheddar cheese, shredded
Salt and pepper to taste

Mix the cubed bread with the beaten eggs, and add the milk, salt, and pepper. Stir in the remaining ingredients, blending well. Pour the mixture into a buttered 2-quart baking dish, and bake for 40 minutes. Wrap in heavy-duty aluminum foil, pack in a Styrofoam cooler, and take to your brunch on the beach.

Serves 4–6

Carla

Ever since I lived in England, I have loved teatime and have had many a tea party back home in Nantucket. However, I think the best tea party was the one I had on the beach. We set up tables with heirloom embroidered linens from my English shop and did flower arrangements in old transferware wash bowls and sugar bowls. It was such a pretty day, nice and warm, and we not only served hot tea and iced tea but also a little Pimm's mixed with lemon and lime soda and, of course, garnished with cucumber! We started our teatime at the proper time of 4:00 p.m. This sandwich recipe is one of the favorites.

2 ounces Stilton cheese or crumbled blue cheese
1 tablespoon dry sherry
2 tablespoons sour cream
3 ounces cream cheese, softened
8 slices very thin white or wheat bread, crusts removed
Black pepper
1 1/2 cups minced watercress

Cream the Stilton or blue cheese, sherry, sour cream, and cream cheese together, and spread the mixture on four slices of the bread. Sprinkle with a little black pepper and place the watercress on top. Put the other slices of bread on top and cut diagonally into fourths, or use cookie cutters to cut into fun shapes.

Serves 6

Carla

The secret to these little delights is to serve them on homemade pumpkin bread. Whenever my mom comes for a visit, she always brings a loaf of her homemade pumpkin bread, which we all enjoy, especially my daughter, Heather. There are box mixes of pumpkin bread that are very good, or sometimes you can buy a loaf at a bakery. The good thing about these sandwiches is they do not get soggy as quickly and can be made up earlier than ones on regular bread.

6 ounces cream cheese, softened
3 ounces dried pitted dates, chopped
Loaf of pumpkin bread, sliced as thinly as possible
4 tablespoons unsalted butter, softened

Chop the dates very fine, and mix them well with the cream cheese. Spread the pumpkin bread with the butter and then spread the cream cheese mixture on half of the bread. Place the other slices on top to make sandwiches. Slice in half for proper-sized tea sandwiches.

Serves 6

This is our take on a chicken salad served in a nearby Providence restaurant. The taste of the garlic and olives is excellent when paired with the creamy chicken salad. Because the olives are very salty, you don't need much salt in the chicken salad.

2 boneless chicken breasts
1/2 cup mayonnaise
1/3 cup fresh dill, chopped
Salt and pepper
1/2 cup green olives
1 clove garlic
Thinly sliced white bread

Poach chicken breasts, cool and shred. Add mayonnaise and chopped fresh dill, and mix well. Season with salt and freshly ground pepper.

Chop olives and garlic in food processor. Spread a layer of the olive paste on the white bread. Add the chicken salad, and top with a second slice. Quarter the sandwiches and serve.

Serves 6

This recipe just happened one day when we were experimenting with different flavors combined with the cucumbers, and it has remained a favorite of ours. We have tried many ways of making the sandwiches up ahead of time, but we find they get soggy and really prefer to do them a couple of hours before serving and covering them well with wax paper in a closed plastic container.

1/2 cup mayonnaise
1/2 cup sour cream
1 tablespoon horseradish
2 tablespoons fresh dill, chopped
1 cucumber, peeled and sliced thinly
8 slices very thin white or wheat bread, crust removed
Freshly ground pepper (to taste)

Mix the first five ingredients together in a medium-sized bowl. Spread the mixture thinly on all eight slices of bread. Place the sliced cucumber on four slices of bread, then place the tops on. While you can cut the bread into any shape, I prefer a round cookie cutter to go with the shape of the cucumber.

Serves 6

At every teatime, there is always an egg salad sandwich, and this one takes first prize because of its curry flavor. You can always add a little chopped green onion or celery, which provides more texture and punch.

4 eggs, hard boiled
1/4 cup mayonnaise
1/2 teaspoon curry powder
1/2 teaspoon Dijon-style mustard
8 slices very thin wheat or white bread
4 tablespoons unsalted butter, softened
Dash of cayenne pepper
Salt (to taste)

In a bowl, chop the eggs, add the mayonnaise, curry powder, and mustard, and mix well. Add the cayenne and salt. Spread the butter on the slices of bread and then spread the egg mixture on four of the slices. Put the other four slices on top to make the sandwich. Cut the sandwiches in triangles, rounds, or finger shapes.

Serves 6

The combination of the ham and pineapple makes one think of a Hawaiian island, and so, being on the island of Nantucket, these sandwiches fit in very well. They are also a little different from the traditional tea sandwiches.

1 cup ground ham
1/2 cup drained, crushed pineapple
1/4 cup chopped green pepper
1 tablespoon brown sugar
1/8 teaspoon ground cloves
8 slices very thin white or wheat
  bread, crusts removed

Mix the first five ingredients together and spread on four slices of the bread. Top with the other four slices of bread, and cut into proper teatime servings.

Serves 6

One of our favorite herbs is rosemary, and we grow big pots of it on our decks every summer. This year we brought the plants in through the winter months; they survived and made our kitchens smell ever so fragrant. For years we have made chicken salad with curry, but adding the rosemary really seems to give it wonderful flavor.

2 1/2 cups cooked chicken, shredded
1/4 cup mayonnaise
1/4 cup sour cream
2 teaspoon minced fresh rosemary
1/4 cup chopped green onion
1 teaspoon curry powder
Salt and pepper (to taste)
8 slices very thin wheat bread, crusts removed
4 tablespoon unsalted butter, softened
1 teaspoon Dijon mustard

In a mixing bowl, combine the first eight ingredients, and mix together well. In another bowl, combine the butter with the mustard and mix well. Spread all eight slices of bread with this mustard butter and then spread the chicken salad mixture on four slices of the bread. Top with the other slices of bread, and cut each sandwich into four triangles.

21 Federal Chili 116

Bridesmaids' Lunch 88

Butterflied Leg of Lamb #1 112

Butterflied Leg of Lamb #2 113

Chicken Cooked under a Brick 95

Chicken Gai Yang 92

Chutney Chicken Salad 91

Dinner with the Banshees 103

Grilled Chicken Breasts with Fresh Tomatoes 96

Grilled Chicken with Capers and Prunes 98

Grilled Duck Breast with Asian Marinade 104

Grilled Meatloaf 105

Heirloom Tomato Pie 90

Italian Zucchini Pie 89

Lamb and White Bean Salad 115

Lamb Burgers with Feta 114

Moonlight Madness 118

Orange Rosemary Pork Chops 106

Sticky Chicky 99

Surprise Burgers 120

Sweet-and-Sour Pork Tenderloins 109

Sweet-and-Spicy Pork Tenderloins 110

Teriyaki Chicken Burgers 100

Teriyaki Marinade 123

Turkey Tostada Salad 101

Veal Chops with Herb Butter 121

BRIDESMAIDS' LUNCH

Carla

One of my favorite things to do is to give bridesmaids' luncheons. There are so many brides who love Nantucket and choose to be married here. We have found a beach party to be a relaxed and appropriate way to celebrate the friendship of the bridesmaids on the beach. This quiche recipe was handed down by my mother and has always been very popular at these celebrations. The great thing about this recipe is that the quiche bakes up nice and firm, which makes it very easy to serve by the seaside. This is one occasion where we pull out all the stops on decorating at the beach, which can be seen in the photo.

Serves 8

Preheat oven to 375°

4 cups thinly sliced, unpeeled zucchini
1/2 cup margarine or butter
1/2 cup chopped parsley
1/2 teaspoon salt
1/2 teaspoon black pepper
1/4 teaspoon garlic powder
1/4 teaspoon sweet basil leaves
1/4 teaspoon oregano leaves
2 eggs, well beaten
8 ounces shredded mozzarella cheese
1 package Pillsbury Ready-Made Crust
2 teaspoons Dijon mustard

In a skillet, cook zucchini and onion in margarine or butter until tender, about 10 minutes. Stir in parsley and seasonings. In a large bowl, blend eggs and cheese. Stir into vegetable mixture. Place crust in pie plate or quiche dish, spread with mustard, and then pour quiche mixture in.

Bake for 18–20 minutes. It is done when the knife comes out clean.

Wrap in a dish towel and then again in foil, place in a Styrofoam cooler (which is great for keeping things hot), and take to your luncheon to the beach.

We usually serve this with a green salad and some fresh fruits.

Each pie serves 4

One summer, when we had our own garden, we grew eight varieties of heirloom tomatoes. Knowing how much we'd love their flavor in the dead of winter, we made a batch of pies and froze them. Come January, we were transported to sunny summer days. These pies are delicious as a side dish or main course at a luncheon, and with frozen pie shells available in any supermarket freezer, they can easily be made in groups of three.

Preheat oven to 375°

10 ripe heirloom tomatoes, sliced
Kosher salt
3 frozen pie crusts
6 eggs
2 cups light cream
1 bag shredded Swiss cheese
1 bunch basil, chopped
1 bunch chives, chopped
Salt and pepper

Slice tomatoes and salt liberally. Allow to sit for 20 minutes and pour off juice that develops. Arrange tomatoes in pie crusts, and grind some fresh pepper onto them.

In a separate bowl, add eggs and beat. Add cheese and herbs. Pour in cream and stir. Pour over tomatoes. Bake for about half an hour until set and browned on top.

Note: You can easily change the flavor of these pies with seasonings. If you add chili powder and jalapenos to the ingredients, you have a Tex-Mex flavor; if you substitute Swiss cheese for cheddar and add chopped onion and thyme, you have a milder French flavor. Use your imagination and see what works.

CHUTNEY CHICKEN SALAD

Serves 2

Sometimes we want to skip the grilling and simply eat dinner on the beach. This is no problem as we have a full complement of salad ideas that make for a fresh and guiltless meal. This chicken salad is spectacular and fairly unusual. It goes fast, so double or triple the recipe if you are serving a lot of people.

1 skinless, boneless chicken breast
1 rib celery, chopped
1 scallion, chopped
2 tablespoons chutney
1/3 cup mayonnaise
Salt and pepper
2 tablespoons slivered almonds

Poach chicken breasts gently in water. Remove and cool. Shred chicken into a bowl and add chopped celery and scallion. Combine mayonnaise and chutney and pour over chicken, stirring. Season to taste. Add almonds and stir.

Serves 8

Deborah

I first had this dish in New York City over a quarter-century ago, when its flavors were so new to my palate that they exploded in my mouth. The restaurant was called CORIANDER, now long closed, and for years I tried to track down the recipe. When I was working at NBC News in New York, we did a piece on local food, and I was able to persuade Chef Joel Levy to tell us his secret ingredient, which, not surprisingly, was coriander, or, as we know it, cilantro. Since his recipe said cilantro was optional, I made the dish without and couldn't understand what was missing. Finally, I got the cilantro, which was still a rare find back then, and it all came together. Simple, still mouth watering, never not a hit. Try it and see, but you will need wet wipes for your sticky fingers, and, certainly, you will need cilantro.

2 chickens, split

Marinade
1 cup soy sauce
6 cloves garlic, crushed
2/3 cup honey or sugar

Heat ingredients until honey is incorporated. Cool to room temperature and pour over chicken. Marinate for 2 hours at room temperature. Grill chickens over coals until they are crisp and release easily. Turn and move to side of grill and cook slowly for another 20 minutes. Drizzle chicken with dipping sauce.

Dipping sauce
1/2 cup cider vinegar
1/2 cup nam pla, or fish sauce
1/2 cup honey
1 tablespoon garlic, finely chopped
1 teaspoon crushed red pepper
2 scallions, finely sliced
1 tablespoon chopped cilantro (not optional)

Combine all ingredients, except scallions and coriander. Bring to a boil and simmer for 5 minutes. Cool and add remaining ingredients. It is important to taste the sauce and make proper adjustments.

GRILLING TECHNIQUES AND TIPS

Keep grill clean, and oil it before each use.

Turn lava rocks on gas grills when drippings accumulate.

When using charcoal, do not begin cooking until the coals are covered in ash.

Brush food lightly with oil before putting on grill.

Brush tin foil lightly with oil before cooking fish or packets.

Keep the cover down on gas grills, up on charcoal grills, for best results.

Add moistened herbs like rosemary or thyme to coals before cooking.

Cook over different woods or add them to your fire for more flavor.

Bring meats to room temperature before grilling, which allows you easier cooking-time calculation.

Let the meat finish cooking on one side until it releases on its own before turning. When meat, poultry, or fish is adequately seared, it will seal and release easily from the grill. If you try to turn it too soon, it will stick and tear.

The second side always takes less time.

When grilling delicate foods, move them to the side after initial searing.

Serves 6

This is an Italian dish, a highlight at trattorias in northern Italy, and particularly in Emilia-Romagna. It can be simple or complex, depending on the herbs you choose to use and the finishing touches. We like to use rosemary, garlic, and lemon. You should end up with a very flavorful, crispy chicken that is excellent served warm or at room temperature. This can easily be prepared in advance and taken to the picnic.

**1 3/4 pound chicken, with backbone cracked
  and flattened out
2 sprigs rosemary, chopped
2 cloves garlic, chopped
1/4 teaspoon salt
1/4 cup extra virgin olive oil
Freshly ground pepper
One lemon, zested and juiced**

Chop rosemary, garlic, lemon zest, salt, and pepper together, making a paste. Take flattened chicken and gently loosen skin from breast meat. Stuff the paste under the skin, flattening it out as you go. Take any extra paste and spread it onto the legs. Season the outside with salt and pepper. Pour olive oil into a large pan and lay chicken in breast side down. Cover with sheet of tin foil and place a heavy cast-iron pot on top of the foil, weighing it down. Cook over medium heat for 12 minutes and turn with tongs. Lower heat, recover with foil and heavy pan, and cook for another 15 minutes. Pierce thigh with fork and check to see if juices run clear. If not, replace pan and cook longer.

When chicken is done, put on a platter, squeeze lemon juice all over, and cover with foil. Tip on angle with breast meat down so juices run back into the chicken. Serve chicken at room temperature or rewarm over coals, watching that it does not burn.

Serves 4

In high summer, when tomatoes are at their most irresistible, this is a surprisingly exciting dish. It is simple and totally healthful and makes great use of summer's bounty.

4 boneless chicken breasts
1/2 cup olive oil
1/2 cup lemon juice
2 cloves garlic, minced
Salt and pepper to taste

Tomatoes:
1 pint cherry tomatoes
Kosher salt
Fresh basil, julienned
4 ounces goat cheese
4 ounces extra virgin olive oil
Freshly ground pepper

Place chicken breasts into a Ziploc bag and add the first five ingredients. Shake and marinate until ready to grill. Slice cherry tomatoes in half and liberally sprinkle with kosher salt. Rest.

After at least a half-hour, pour 4 ounces extra virgin olive oil on tomatoes. Add julienned basil and crumbled goat cheese. Stir.

Grill chicken breasts about 5 minutes per side. Top with several tablespoons of tomato mixture. Serve.

GUIDE TO AROMATIC WOODS

Adding different woods to your fire will dramatically alter flavor. Most of us are familiar with mesquite, which is used in Western barbecues and evokes the image of the chuck wagon, but many other woods are available from specialty food stores that will please your palate. Fruit woods like apple and cherry will make poultry and fish a little sweeter and add a slightly smoky taste. Grapevines, commonly used in Europe and California, burn very hot and add great taste to steaks and chops. Oak is wonderful for large pieces of meat that cook slowly, but in the process it does add a very smoky taste.

Serves 6

This is our take on the once ubiquitous Chicken Marbella that seemed to turn up at every dinner party in the Eighties. We have taken the original recipe, which came from the *Silver Palate Cookbook*, and made it more user-friendly. What you end up with is a flavorful, juicy chicken breast that can be served at a contemporary dinner party alongside a simple pesto pasta and a Caesar salad. Because the chicken marinates after grilling, it remains moist and works as a topping to a green salad or as the main ingredient in a chicken salad. We think this recipe retains all that was great about the original, and makes it a possible last-minute dish. It's fine to serve this at room temperature.

6 boneless chicken breasts
6 cloves garlic, chopped
2 teaspoons dried oregano
1/4 cup red wine vinegar
1/4 cup olive oil
1/2 cup pitted prunes
1/2 cup pitted green olives
2 tablespoons capers
1/2 cup brown sugar
1/2 cup white wine
Extra virgin olive oil
Salt and pepper
Fresh cilantro, chopped

Brush chicken breasts with extra virgin olive oil and grill over hot coals for about 4 minutes per side, or until chicken feels somewhat firm and appears almost cooked through. It will continue to cook in the marinade. Put all other ingredients into a saucepan and heat gently for about 5 minutes, allowing sugar to melt and wine to burn off its alcohol. Cool. Slice cooled chicken and put into a Ziploc bag. Pour sauce over chicken and seal bag. Remove when ready to serve, and garnish with chopped cilantro.

Serves 4

This is one of those intriguing recipes that turned out to be better than imagined. Sticky, sweet, delicious. We like to serve it with rice that sops up the sauce and Asian Slaw. The chicken is great any time, but particularly wonderful at the beach, where you can run down to the water and rinse off your fingers, as you will dip into every ounce of the sauce. Also, another bonus, it can all be done ahead and served at room temperature or reheated briefly on the grill. If you do prepare it at home, make sure you include all the sauce in the roasting pan for the final presentation.

Preheat oven 450°

1 chicken, cut into 8 pieces
3 scallions, cut into thin slivers, including green tops

Marinade
1 can coconut milk
2 tablespoons minced ginger
1 teaspoon pepper
1 teaspoon hot pepper flakes (optional)

Glaze
3/4 cup rice vinegar
1/2 cup sugar
3 tablespoons soy sauce
1 teaspoon hot pepper flakes (optional)

Combine marinade ingredients and pour over chicken in covered container or Ziploc bag. Marinate overnight, or for at least three hours at room temperature. Remove chicken and reserve marinade. Grill over high heat on gas grill with lid closed, or over regular coals, basting with marinade and turning to avoid burning. Cook on grill for about 10 - 15 minutes. Remove to roasting pan. Prepare glazing sauce and pour over chicken before roasting for another10 minutes in the oven.

When ready to serve, plate chicken and pour pan drippings over chicken. Garnish with green onions.

Serves 4

The fresh ginger gives this burger a very unusual flavor, and it works well with ground beef or ground turkey.

1 pound boneless, skinless chicken breasts
2 tablespoons soy sauce
1 teaspoon salt
1 teaspoon fresh ginger, minced
1 clove garlic, minced

Grind raw chicken breasts in the food processor. Add all ingredients and pulse several times until mixed. Shape into 4 patties.

Grill over gray coals approximately 5 · 7 minutes, turning once.

Serve on toasted buns.

Serves 4

We ordered a version of this salad when we were in Santa Monica at the Border Café, and it appealed totally because it was fresh, healthy, and had many sources of flavor. Since then we have started making our own version. This is a great picnic item as the salad can be assembled at home and the dressing added at the beach. The tostadas are available at Stop and Shop, but if you can't find them, it is easy enough to crisp up your own corn tortillas to finish the salad, and if all else fails, add tortilla chips at the end. This is a perfect summer lunch or light dinner.

1 head of romaine lettuce, rinsed and chopped
12 cherry tomatoes, halved
2/3 cup red onion, chopped
1 cup shredded cheddar cheese
2 avocados chopped
1 bunch cilantro, chopped
8 ounces turkey breast, cut into 1/2-inch cubes
Salt and pepper
1/2 cup olive oil
1/3 cup red wine vinegar
Corn tostadas

Put the first seven ingredients into a large plastic bag and bring to the beach. When you get there, throw them into a bowl and salt and pepper to taste. Add oil and vinegar and toss. Put one or two corn tostados onto a plate and top with salad.

Note: You can customize this salad by adding corn or black beans, making it even more filling. One way or another, beyond the 60 calories in the corn tostada, this is healthy, low-cal food.

Serves 4

Deborah

Chef Michael Shannon became one of my dearest friends during my years in Nantucket. I had been crazy wild about his cooking since I met him when I was pregnant with my oldest child. Up until then, absolutely nothing had tasted good or stayed down, until we drove by the Harbor House one spring weekend and saw a sign saying he was the chef. My ex-husband had worked with him in Vermont, and so we went in to try his food. Wouldn't you know, I couldn't eat boiled chicken, but had no problem with rich French sauces. I not only digested it, I adored it. From that point on, I was his devotee, stopping in his kitchens, sampling items, and bringing home his precious meat glaze, which I would pour into ice trays and use all winter. He would always drop off a quart of his amazing clam chowder when my Dad and Mom came to the island. He was generous enough to prepare a feast for about two dozen friends for my 50th birthday, and I had him back to Providence for dinner at my house with his idol, Julia Child.

But when I was in Nantucket, the only way I could repay him was to make him dinner. He was too tired from cooking at the Club Car to make his own dinner. He ate at the house many times, but often I would take the dinner over with my little girls and drop it at his neighboring Vestal Street home. The girls knew he was terrified of the Irish banshees, so they would hide under his windows and make howling noises, scaring absolutely no one. This was one of his favorite dinners, and it definitely works at a beach picnic.

1 pork tenderloin
3 cloves garlic, chopped
1/4 cup olive oil
1/4 cup balsamic vinegar
2 tablespoons Dijon mustard, preferably Maille
1/4 cup fresh rosemary, chopped
Salt and pepper

Marinate pork in above ingredients for at least 3 hours, or overnight. Grill tenderloins over hot coals, and when finished, pour marinade over cooked meat. Grill tenderloin over hot coals, turning several times. They will cook within 15 minutes. When finished, rest 5 minutes, slice, and pour marinade over slices.

Serves 8

Deborah

One weekend when Michael Shannon was considering joining us at a beach picnic, he marinated some Muscovy duck breasts. At the last minute, he could not come, but he sent along the duck. We were the envy of all the other picnickers, and even though Michael does not remember exactly what was in the marinade, he helped me come up with the general idea. This works on all duck breasts and makes for a succulent, flavorful entrée.

4 duck breasts
1/2 cup orange juice
2 tablespoons orange zest
1 cup soy sauce
1/2 cup olive oil
1/2 cup sesame oil
1/2 cup rice wine
1/2 cup rice wine vinegar
1 tablespoon chopped fresh garlic
1 tablespoon chopped fresh ginger
1/3 cup Rose's lime juice
1 fresh lime, juiced
Crushed Szechuan pepper to taste

Score duck skin in cross pattern, making sure not to cut through to the flesh. Mix marinade ingredients and pour over duck breasts. Marinate at least 6 hours, or overnight, to maximize flavor. Marinating any longer than overnight breaks down the duck flesh and begins the cooking process, so don't do that. When ready to grill, place duck breasts skin side down. Duck fat renders quickly and will flame up. Cooking on the outside edge of the grill will be more manageable. When the first side looks well crisped, turn with tongs and cook on other side for about 5 minutes. Rest for 5 minutes, slice, and serve.

Serves 8

If you like meatloaf, then you will love this one done on the grill. It is perfect for a September picnic, when it starts to cool down at the end of the day, and the air is so crisp. This is one you must prepare at home and bring to the beach to cook.

3 pounds ground beef
1 onion, finely chopped
2/3 cup tomato paste
1 cup bread crumbs
8 ounces grated cheddar cheese
1/2 cup chopped parsley leaves
2 eggs, beaten
2 teaspoons salt
1 teaspoon freshly ground pepper

In a bowl, combine the chopped onion, beef, tomato paste, bread crumbs, cheddar cheese, parsley, eggs, salt, and pepper. Shape into a large loaf and wrap tightly in two sheets of heavy-duty aluminum foil. Heat the grill until coals are medium gray, and there are no flames. Place on the grill and turn over every 8–10 minutes for approximately 45 minutes.

Remove from the grill, open the aluminum packet, and slice the meatloaf. Put the slices back on the grill for a quick grilling on each side. Serve with homemade potato salad and nice, fresh, end-of-the-summer tomatoes.

Serves 6

Grilling pork chops brings out an entirely different flavor than does roasting or panfrying. These chops are particularly juicy after an overnight brining. The topping of flavored butter adds to the fresh outdoor appeal. Again, this is an easy dish to prepare, and it is perfect at a picnic. The grilling is a no-brainer, but the sauce rendered from the herb butter makes it feel like a restaurant meal.

6 thick pork chops
3 quarts water
1/2 cup kosher salt
1/2 cup sugar

Bring water to boil and add sugar until it melts. Add salt and stir until dissolved. Add several cups of ice cubes to cool. Pour cool brine into container or bag and add chops. Seal and brine overnight.

Herb Butter
Zest of one orange
Leaves from 1 sprig of fresh rosemary
1 large shallot
1 stick softened salted butter
1/2 cup fresh orange juice
2 tablespoons pepper jelly

Place first three ingredients in food processor and chop. Add softened butter, juice, and pepper jelly and pulse to incorporate. Roll into log and chill.

Grill chops over charcoal. Remove and top with 1 tablespoon herb butter. Allow to rest and serve.

ANNYE'S WHOLE FOODS

In the six years since Annye's Whole Foods has been opened, it has become a great resource for all of our picnics. Annye Camara, who has now expanded her store in a new location on Amelia Drive, offers the freshest organic ingredients and the most acclaimed meats and poultry. Annye's is one of those wonderful stores you want to linger in, because there is so much appeal. We love the artisan cheeses and the assortment of crackers; we love the chickens she imports from the Canadian farmer who uses organic feed. We can find our Muscovy duck here and even a great wine to drink with it. We used to have to order from New York if we wanted D'Artagnan poultry or Niman Ranch beef and pork, but now she has brought these foods to Nantucket, and we are thrilled. Annye's also has magnificent produce, much of it organic. When we are feeling especially lazy, we also turn to Annye's for takeout picnics, like lamb riblets or chicken pot pies. For us, it is perfect one-stop shopping with a parking space.

SAND PAIL PICNICS

For a special occasion on the beach, such as a birthday party, it is fun to buy plastic sand pails in bright colors with the shovel attached to the handle. The sand pails are good for holding a sandwich-type picnic with chips, fruit and a drink, all wrapped in cellophane. You can write each person's name on the attached shovel, and it becomes an instant party favor. Really fun!!

Serves 2

We love pork tenderloins because they are grill-friendly and can take on as many identities as chicken does. This dish is marinated for a day, and then the marinade is poured off and reduced until it makes a thickened sauce. It is tangy and sweet and is marvelous accompanied by the Cheddar Chili Corn. If you are making more than one tenderloin, double the sauce ingredients because the sauce makes the dish.

1 12-ounce pork tenderloin
2/3 cup fresh lemon juice
1/3 cup soy sauce
6 tablespoons honey
1/4 cup chopped shallots
3 cloves garlic, chopped
1 tablespoon salt
1 teaspoon pepper
1 teaspoon powdered ginger
1 teaspoon dry mustard
1 bay leaf

Put pork tenderloin and all other ingredients in a Ziploc bag and marinate overnight. Before leaving for the beach, pour the marinade into a saucepan, and bring to a boil. Lower the temperature and cook about 5 minutes or until it reaches a thicker, saucelike consistency. Pour sauce into container and take to the beach along with the pork. Grill the tenderloin, turning often until it is cooked to your liking, about 20 minutes. Slice and serve with sauce.

Serves 6

This is another version of pork tenderloin. We think of this one as a shish kabob without the skewers.

2 12–16 ounce pork tenderloins
2 ears of corn, husked and washed
1 red onion, cut into wedges
1 pound yellow squash, cut in half lengthwise
1 green pepper, cut into quarters
1 red pepper, cut into quarters
1 cup favorite barbeque sauce
1/2 cup honey mustard
1 teaspoon crushed red pepper
2 teaspoon dried sage, crushed
Salt and freshly ground pepper to taste

Cut each tenderloin into four pieces and sprinkle with salt and pepper. Prepare the vegetables and sprinkle them with salt and pepper. Combine the barbeque sauce, honey mustard, crushed red pepper, and sage in a bowl and divide in half. Arrange the coals for indirect grilling, putting an aluminum foil drip pan in the middle. Place the pork tenderloin on the grill over the drip pan, cover, and grill for 35–40 minutes. Arrange the vegetables around the edge of the grill for the last 20 minutes of cooking, and during the last 10 minutes of cooking, brush the pork and vegetables with the barbeque mixture. To serve, cut all vegetables and pork into bite· size pieces, and serve with the remaining sauce, which has been heated in a pan on the grill.

INDIRECT GRILLING

Indirect grilling is a great way to grill large cuts of meat or whole chickens. The food is positioned on the grill away from the burning charcoal. The best way to do this is to light the coals and, after they have died down a bit, to push the coals to the sides of the grill, leaving an empty space in the middle. This allows the food to cook slowly without any flare-ups.

PICNIC CENTERPIECE

When the children were young, we would pick a few flowers from the garden at home and put them in water in a mayonnaise jar and take them off to the beach. When we arrived at the beach, we would ask the children to go looking for driftwood, shells, beach glass, stones and even dried seaweed to make the centerpiece for our picnic table. They had such fun running all over the beach looking for things and even more fun being crafty back at the picnic table. Some of the arrangements were marvelous, and this provided a good activity for the children while the adults were getting set up.

Serves 6–8

Carla

Our family lived in England for five years back in the 1990's. A good friend shared this lamb recipe with me. It was a good dish over in the U.K., where lambs are plentiful, and you can count on absolute freshness. Because the lamb was so delicious, and beef was less available, we prepared it in many different ways. This is a recipe we keep using today.

6–8 pound leg of lamb, butterflied
4 cloves garlic, minced
2/3 cup lemon juice
1/3 cup dry white vermouth
1 tablespoon rosemary
1 teaspoon salt
1 teaspoon pepper
1/4 cup olive oil
1/4 cup Worcestershire sauce
2/3 cup Dijon mustard
1 tablespoon rosemary

Make marinade by combining garlic, lemon juice, vermouth, rosemary, salt, pepper, olive oil, and Worcestershire sauce. Marinate lamb for 24 hours in refrigerator, turning several times. Place rosemary on the coals. Cook lamb for 20 minutes on each side, brushing the surface with the marinade and the Dijon mustard.

Serves 10

This is a great dish to cook for a crowd. The boned lamb varies in thickness throughout, which makes it easy to accommodate the various preferences of rare versus well done in your crowd. The marinade on this will caramelize and add a delicious crunch to each bite. Also, because it is lamb and not poultry, it is fine to put the cooked lamb back into the marinade after grilling so that there is a delicious sauce for each person. If this becomes a repeat recipe, which we suspect it will, you might want to double the amount of the marinade for use on leftovers and sliced lamb. This lamb is also wonderful in a salad the next day, with red onions and feta cheese and a vinaigrette mixed with the remaining marinade.

1 boned lamb leg, fell* removed
1/2 cup soy sauce
1/2 cup olive oil
1/2 cup brown sugar
4 tablespoons Dijon mustard
1/4 cup honey
6 garlic cloves, crushed
2 sprigs fresh rosemary (2 tablespoons dried rosemary)

Place all marinade ingredients in a saucepan and bring to a slow boil. Lower heat and cook several minutes to allow sugar to melt. Cool. Pour over lamb and marinate for several hours in a Ziploc bag.

Remove lamb from the bag, retaining the marinade. Place lamb over center of coals, and cook until lamb releases from grill—about 6 minutes. Turn and sear the other side. Move lamb to side of grill and cook for 10–15 minutes. Test with touch. Rare lamb will be softer, despite caramelized crust. Medium will be more resistant to the touch. Feel free to remove the lamb to a carving board and slice into the thickest piece. That will allow you to gauge the doneness. When ready, slice and pour marinade over lamb. This lamb is great served hot or at room temperature.

*The fell is the thin membrane that covers the lamb.

Serves 6

It is fun to play with different burger options, and this is one of our favorite versions. Lamb has so much flavor, and enhanced by the herbs and lemon, it is even better. Try mixing the feta into the lamb as you make the burgers. Play with the mayo, and add in different herbs until you find your favorite. Use good crusty rolls, top with sliced, grilled red onion and mayo, and serve.

2 pounds ground lamb
3 cloves garlic chopped
1/2 cup chopped mint
1 tablespoon oregano
Juice of one lemon
Salt and freshly ground pepper
1 cup feta cheese, crumbled
Red onions, sliced
Hard roll or French bread
1 cup mayonnaise
2/3 cup fresh dill, chopped
1/2 teaspoon garlic salt

Mix first six ingredients together in bowl. Incorporate feta into mixture. Form burgers. Mix chopped fresh dill into mayonnaise. Grill burgers and red onions. Grill split rolls or French bread. Assemble each burger and top with mayo and onion. Grill burgers for about 6 minutes per side.

Serves 2

Deborah

Roy Bailey was such a great friend that when he finally tired of escorting just about every single woman on Nantucket to various events, he asked me to help him find "a babe." I did. He came to Providence one fall day, and at a dinner party with several single women, he met Nancy Verde Barr. Nancy had been Julia Child's executive chef for several years and is the author of two best-selling cookbooks. For Roy and Nancy, the chemistry was instantaneous, and they ultimately married. Nancy moved to Nantucket shortly after they met, and the two of them spent every day together until Roy died a few years ago. Nancy and I have spent years talking food, and she graciously supplied several recipes for this book. This is one of her favorites.

1/2 cup red wine vinegar
1/4 cup fresh mint, chopped
1 tablespoon fresh thyme, chopped
1 1/2 cups virgin olive oil
12 thin slices cooked lamb, trimmed of fat
1 1/2 cup dried white beans
1 ham bone
1 red onion, split
1/2 cup parsley, chopped
1/4 cup sun-dried tomatoes, oil packed, julienned
Salt and pepper

Place vinegar, mint, thyme, salt, and pepper in blender. Slowly add olive oil, making a thick dressing. Place lamb slices in shallow nonreactive bowl and cover with 3/4 cup of the dressing. Cover and refrigerate to marinate overnight. Rinse dried beans and remove any foreign particles. Cover with cold water by at least 1 inch and leave to soak overnight. Drain. In a large pot, cover beans with water by at least 2 inches. Add bone. Bring to a boil and skim off any foam that rises. Reduce heat to moderate and cover, cooking for about 40 minutes. Drain and remove bone.

Toss hot beans with remaining cup of dressing. Mince half the red onion and add to beans with salt, pepper, and chopped parsley. Set aside to cool to room temperature. Slice remaining half-onion into thin rings and soak in cold water for 1 hour to sweeten. Change the water three times during the hour. Spread the beans onto a platter. Top with lamb slices, onion rings, and sun-dried tomatoes.

Serves 12

Deborah

When 21 Federal opened its doors twenty-one years ago, it quickly became my favorite restaurant in the world. Chef Bob Kinkead turned out amazing dishes, each more delectable than the last. When we came back to Nantucket in the fall and winter, we would hit 21 Federal for lunch and dinner. One especially cold November day, we had a bowl of the best chili I have ever tasted.

I was able to persuade the chef to give me the ingredients, which are plentiful. It is a long recipe, but well worth the trouble.

Note: this is even better if you happen to be using already-grilled meat, which is more available during the summer. Rest assured, it works splendidly with regularly prepared meats.

1/2 pound bacon
2 onions
2 red peppers
2 green peppers
4 stalks celery, diced
4 jalapeno peppers, chopped
1 pound lamb, boneless stew meat
1 pound beef chuck
1 pound pork, boneless
1 pound veal, stew cut
1 tablespoon chili powder
1 tablespoon thyme
1 tablespoon cumin
1 tablespoon coriander seed
1 tablespoon oregano
1/4 cup masa (corn meal)
1 28-ounce can crushed tomatoes

5 tomatillos, sautéed and chopped
2 cans diced green chilies
4 cloves garlic, chopped
Juice of one lime
1 cup orange juice
28 ounces beef stock
1 ounce unsweetened chocolate
Sour cream
Shredded cheddar cheese
Scallions, chopped
Cayenne pepper to taste
Salt and pepper

Sauté bacon and remove from pan. Drain on paper towels, crumble, and reserve In bacon grease, sauté onions, celery, chilies. Remove from pan.

Add diced meat and brown.

In a separate pan, blacken spices and grind them fine. Add to meat and cook for 20 minutes over medium-low heat.

Add bacon. Add corn meal. Stir and add crushed tomatoes. Add diced green chilies and tomatillos. Add lime and orange juice Add stock, garlic, and unsweetened chocolate.

Simmer for 2 hours.

Serve with chopped scallions, shredded cheddar cheese, and sour cream.

Serves 4–6

Every year, when there is a full midsummer moon, the Nantucket Yacht Club organizes a sailboat race from the committee boat to Pocomo Point. The boats start out at dusk and race up harbor to the sandy beach where food and drink are waiting. After wading to shore and having a feast, the sailors head back home, hoping the wind will hold until they make their moorings. Spirits are high, the nights are magic, and the food waiting at the end of a brisk sail is—not surprisingly—enjoyed with great gusto. Here is a recipe we made one moonlit night, which will prove it was not just the worked up appetites, but the quality and flavor of what we offered, that made the food so memorable.

Steak
2 pounds skirt steak
Salt and pepper

Skirt steak is a great cut of meat, cooks quickly, and is juicy and very flavorful. You only need to season with salt and pepper and grill for 3 or 4 minutes per side.

Sauce
1 tablespoon fish sauce
1 tablespoon sugar
1 teaspoon fresh cracked pepper
1 hot chili, seeded and roughly chopped
2 tablespoons fresh lime juice
2 cloves garlic
2 large shallots
1 half-bunch fresh mint
1 half-bunch fresh cilantro

Combine everything but the mint and cilantro in a food processor and chop finely. Add the washed and dried herbs, and chop again until a fine consistency. Use the sauce to drizzle on the grilled meat. It is so fresh and delicious you will want seconds, and this is an ample amount. We love the hot pepper, but if you want to eliminate the heat, you will find that the sauce stands on its own.

119

Serves 2

This is another great burger presentation. We love this one because it is juicy and moist, and the burst of cheddar cheese oozing in the middle is a great addition. If you prefer blue cheese use that instead of cheddar. We serve this with the Easy Pepper Tomato Relish. Since relish is so easy to make, it is almost a shame to buy it. This is one of our favorite relish recipes not only for its flavor but its crunch. It goes well on burgers, sausages, and hot dogs. When Carla's Dad comes along to a beach picnic, he is always poking around the table to make sure we remembered this relish, and he smiles wide when he finds it.

1 pound ground sirloin
1/2 cup minced Vidalia onion
1 tablespoon Worcestershire sauce
1 tablespoon soy sauce
1 tablespoon A1 Steak Sauce
2 thick slices cheddar cheese

Put ground meat in a bowl and add the first four ingredients. Work them through the meat with your hands. Form burgers, placing a slice of cheddar cheese in the center of each burger. Grill burgers for approximately 5 minutes on the first side, then turn and cook for 3 more minutes for medium rare.

Easy Pepper Tomato Relish
Makes 2 cups

1 cup chopped sweet red pepper
1 cup chopped and seeded red tomato
1 jalapeno pepper, seeded and chopped
1/2 cup chopped red onion
2 tablespoons balsamic vinegar
1/4 teaspoon salt

Combine all the ingredients in a bowl, then cover and chill for 2 hours. Store in a covered jar in refrigerator until ready to use on burgers and dogs.

Serves 4

Veal chops are a great alternative to steak. They work beautifully on the grill, and if you let them rest with a flavorful herb butter, they are juicy and succulent. They are also one of those meats that don't steal the show, allowing the sides, like the green beans with basil, to take center stage. A great veal chop is a first-class meal.

Chops
4 veal chops, each 1 1/2 inches thick
Olive oil
Salt and pepper

Season chops and place on hot grill. Cook on first side for 5 minutes, or until chop releases from grill easily. Turn and cook on second side. You will know the chop is cooked when it is slightly firm to your finger. Best served medium rare. Top with butter of choice and let stand for several minutes until juices are distributed.

Herb Butter
1 tablespoon shallot
1 tablespoon rosemary
1 stick salted butter, softened
1 tablespoon Dijon mustard
1 tablespoon fresh lemon juice
Kosher salt
Freshly ground pepper

Place shallot and rosemary into food processor and pulse until blended. Add butter, mustard, and lemon juice and pulse. Turn herb butter onto parchment paper or waxed paper and roll to form a log. Butter can be frozen and sliced into pats as needed.

Roquefort Herb Butter
1 stick salted butter, softened
2 ounces Roquefort cheese
1 scallion, minced, including green top
1 tablespoon balsamic vinegar or fresh lemon juice

Place all ingredients in food processor and pulse until blended. Put butter onto parchment paper or waxed paper and roll to form a log. Butter can be frozen and sliced into pats as needed.

It seems as though every one who comes to Nantucket shares two common sentiments: they want to possess it, staking every claim, historical and contemporary, to their particular place in the Nantucket cosmos, and each and every person who falls in love with the Gray Lady fancies that he or she might live there year round. Considering that 56,000 step on island in a busy August, and the 2000 census recorded fewer than 5,000 year-round residents, it is clear that the second sentiment has not achieved reality. The first, however, is very real. The island does captivate many people and has for hundreds of years. Nantucket was discovered by Norsemen in the eleventh century, originally populated by Wamponaug Indians, and claimed by the English in the 1600s. Nantucket was finally settled by Thomas Macy and a few other families around 1660, and plenty of contemporary folk trace their roots back to those original Coffins and Swaynes, Mitchells and Pikes. Whether we are related or not, we all revel in the history of the whaling captains, the fire, and the town moving from Capaum Pond to where it sits today. We also cherish our characters, from the Wharf Rats to Gwen Gaillard at the Opera House, from Ted Anderson to Walter Beinecke, from Madaket Millie to Clambo, all of whom have shaped our island. To know about them is to know Nantucket.

Even if we aren't descendants and don't know these names, we all know what it is like to feel the fog, swim in that mighty ocean, and smell the roses. We may be 30 miles out to sea, but we are a worldly sophisticated group who know how to enjoy ourselves, know what we have here is extraordinary, and know that a simple beach picnic is actually an unequalled life experience to be savored and remembered.

Enough for 4 steaks

Carla

Through the years we have tried many different marinades for beef but have always gone back to this wonderful recipe that an American friend in England shared with us. It was a rare treat for us to have beef in the U.K., and many a time a suitcase of beef accompanied us across the Atlantic to our British home. However, getting through security is so difficult today, we do not recommend trying to do this now.

1 cup vegetable oil
1/2 cup soy sauce
1/2 cup teriyaki sauce
8 tablespoons catsup
4 tablespoons red wine vinegar
1 teaspoon freshly ground pepper
8 cloves fresh garlic, crushed

Mix all the ingredients together in medium-sized bowl. This is a great marinade for chicken or beef. It is best to leave the meat in the marinade in the refrigerator for at least 24 hours.

Note: When grilling meats, they can be returned to marinade to rest and create a juice or sauce. Chicken marinade, on the other hand, must be discarded for safety reasons.

SEAFOOD ENTREES

Antipasto Fish Salad 128

Bill Sandole's Simple Fish Salad 130

Crispy Fish with Lemon 129

Grilled Bluefish with Tomato and Fennel 132

Grilled Marinated Shrimp 135

Grilled Oysters 134

Grilled Roasted Fish with Cucumber-Dill Sauce 133

Martini Salmon 137

Swordfish Marinade 136

Toddy's Nantucket Clambake 126

Serves 15

Deborah

When I was 11 years old, my parents rented a house on Brant Point, and that summer, the Andrea Doria sank off Nantucket. I heard about it early in the morning on the radio and got on my bike to go tell my grandparents. Their nephew, Mike Todd, was there. He left immediately and went out to offer rescue assistance. Mike Todd, "Toddy," was a widower who had lost his wife shortly after his daughter was born. Toddy lived in Nantucket nearly all his life, working in salvage, flying his plane, bringing the Nantucket Lightship into the harbor. He was a selectman and a volunteer fireman who kept his boots by the door. He raised his daughter, Heidi, by himself and more than once took her in the truck when he dashed off to the fires. Heidi became the darling of local Nantucketers. When she came to visit us one Christmas, we were amazed by, and a little jealous of, her plethora of Christmas gifts because so many Islanders, loving this motherless child, took the time to give her something. Toddy had a house in town and a little shack in Madaket. When he died, Heidi fixed up that Madaket house and still has it today. She is an accomplished cook, and she has many favorite beach recipes that she serves to her husband and two daughters. One family favorite is her dad's famous clambake.

20 red potatoes
20 ears corn
10 lobsters
3 pounds Italian sausage
10 dozen hard-shell clams, preferably littlenecks or steamers
Seaweed
Melted butter
Lemon wedges

In the old days, this was all about driftwood and bonfires, but using charcoal makes it easier. Dig a pit in the sand, and line it with grates from a grill or oven. Put charcoal on top of the grates. Light the charcoal and cover with more grates or a metal sheet. When the fire is hot, cover the grates with a thin layer of seaweed. Place the potatoes and corn on the seaweed, and cover with another thin layer of seaweed. Lay the sausage and lobsters on top, with more seaweed. Finally, place the clams and mussels and cover with a thick layer of seaweed and a wet tarp that you have soaked in seawater. Keep wetting the tarp, which will steam everything inside. It will take about 1 hour and 15 minutes for the clams to open and the lobsters to turn red. Serve with melted butter, lemon wedges, lobster bibs, and plenty of napkins.

Serves 6

This is one of Nancy Verde Barr Bailey's favorite recipes. She published a version of it in *Food and Wine* over 15 years ago, but she says it was such a successful recipe that she has served it many, many times since. Nancy says this antipasto works well with any leftover firm-fleshed fish that has been grilled or broiled—tuna, swordfish, and mako are all good, as are poached shrimps and scallops.

1/2 cup, plus 3 tablespoons, extra virgin olive oil,
1/2 cup pimentos, drained and finely chopped
1/2 cup parsley, minced
1/4 cup fresh lemon juice
2 large scallions, thinly sliced
2 teaspoons dried oregano
1 tablespoon drained capers, rinsed
1/2 teaspoon salt
1 1/2 pounds fish
1 garlic clove, minced
2 small zucchinis, cut into very thin slices
2 bunches arugula, washed
1/4 pound brine-cured black olives, like Gaeta, for garnish
Lemon slices for garnish

In a small, nonreactive skillet, combine the olive oil with the pickled red peppers, parsley, lemon juice, scallions, oregano, and capers. Heat gently over low heat for about 5 minutes. Season with salt.

In a small skillet, heat the remaining oil with the garlic over moderate heat until garlic is softened but not browned, about 2 minutes. Add zucchini and increase heat to medium high, cooking and stirring until tender. Immediately add the remaining dressing and toss to coat.

Arrange arugula on six small plates. Top with the fish, zucchini, and any residual dressing. Garnish with olives and lemon slices and serve.

Serves 4

With ocean fresh seafood readily available in Nantucket, even at the beach, it is great to have a few simple ways of preparing it. In this dish, the lemon salsa provides a great accent to the fish, and this simple sauce can be used with any thick-skinned fish, like salmon, trout, or snapper.

4 salmon filets, brushed with vegetable oil
Salt and pepper

Lemon Salsa
1 lemon, peeled and thinly sliced
3/4 tablespoon of sugar
1/2 cup chopped chives
1/4 cup capers, drained and rinsed
Salt and pepper

Grill salmon, skin side down, about 4 minutes on the first side. Turn and watch for another couple of minutes. Season with salt and pepper.

Combine lemon, sugar, chives, and capers, and stir to combine. Season with salt and pepper. Top grilled fish with lemon salsa.

Serves 2

When Bill moved to the island in 1977 from Sturbridge, Massachusetts, he started his business selling fish door-to-door to restaurants. He eventually picked up some nonrestaurant customers. For years he did business "out the back door," as he refers to it, and all his customers thought that buying from him that way was their little secret. He gave us this recipe, which he serves with fish, but which can easily be adapted to meats.

2 handfuls field greens (mesclun)
8 ounces mushrooms
4 ounces goat cheese
4 ounces oven-roasted or sun-dried tomatoes
Raspberry vinaigrette dressing
8–10 sprigs fresh tarragon
Fleur de Sel
**Grilled salmon, grilled shrimp, jumbo lump crabmeat,
or tenderloin of beef**

Cut the mushrooms in thumbnail-sized chunks (not slices) and sauté in two parts olive oil to one part butter. Sprinkle lightly with salt, pepper, and hot pepper flakes. About 1 minute before the mushrooms are done, add the tarragon. While still warm, place in a bowl, cover, and set aside.

Toss the greens with just enough dressing to coat THEM and then spread the greens on a flat plate. Crumble goat cheese on top of the greens. Add the mushrooms and then the tomatoes (oven-roasted are preferred). Sprinkle lightly with Fleur de Sel.

For a complete meal, top the salad with grilled salmon, grilled shrimp, jumbo lump crabmeat, or thinly sliced tenderloin of beef. This meal is best served at room temperature.

EAST COAST SEAFOOD
167 Hummock Pond Road

Carla

Whenever we want some nice fresh seafood, we head out to Bill Sandole's 167. We think that Bill is known for having the best fish on the island. He comes from three generations of fine-food purveyors.

On an April day, when I stopped in to see Bill, he was getting ready to open for the season in a few days. The store had been freshly painted and everything was immaculate. When I got back to my shop, I told one of my customers that Bill was going to open in two days. She said she could not wait to finally have some really good seafood after the long winter, and she would be his first customer on opening day. It turns out she was the first....in line. Not only does he have great fish, but we all go because we appreciate that he is such a nice man, a very likable soul.

Serves 4

Among the lasting images of a beach picnic on Great Point are the silhouettes of the fishermen along the shore. From dusk until sundown, they cast their rods, hoping for a run of blues. They can regularly be seen hauling in their fish, filleting it on the spot, and grilling it up for dinner. We're always ready when one of our picnickers is fishing, and here is a simple combination of ingredients to have on hand to make a lovely sauce. We bring these ingredients to almost every picnic, except for the fennel, which pairs beautifully with bluefish, so at the last minute, you can omit the fennel and do quite well.

1 bluefish, cleaned and filleted
1/2 fennel bulb, cut in half and sliced thinly
1/2 onion, sliced
1 tomato, sliced
Salt and pepper
White wine

Place bluefish on a sheet of tin foil, skin side down. Add fennel, onion, and tomato, sprinkle with wine, and fold foil back over to cover. Cook about 15 minutes, and open packet carefully, poking with a knife first to release the steam.

Serves 5

Great on cod, salmon, fresh bluefish, haddock, or just about any fish, this sauce moistens the fish and lends tremendous flavor. We always use foil with this recipe, keeping in all the sauce and basically roasting the fish as you would in the oven.

**1 bunch fresh dill, coarsely chopped
1 cup cucumber, peeled and roughly cubed
3 shallots, roughly chopped
3/4 cup mayonnaise
3/4 cup sour cream
Cayenne pepper to taste**

Combine all ingredients in food processor and chop roughly. Place fish on sheet of foil smothered in sauce (under and over) and seal foil. Place packet on grill and cook until done.

Serves 4

Everyone knows oyster lovers are fanatics and will opt for oysters whenever they are available. They are among the first items to go at raw bars. Instead of eating raw oysters, try grilling them. They are shockingly delicious, and if you cook them correctly, sitting in their juices, they will delight you beyond imagination. You can eat these oysters with a lemon butter or a mignonette sauce, but completely naked, they will do the job. If you serve them with a loaf of bread, a salad, and a jug of wine, you can't do much better.

5 dozen oysters
Butter
Fresh lemon juice

Mignonette Sauce
1 tablespoon coarsely ground white peppercorns
1/2 cup champagne vinegar
2 tablespoons shallots, finely chopped
Salt to taste

When the grill is hot, place oysters flat side up, rounded side down on the grill. The oyster lives in the rounded side, so this assures that it sits in its own juices while it cooks. In 2 or 3 minutes, the oyster shell will open slightly. Remove the oysters to a platter, and when you can handle them, pry them open all the way. Using a small knife, remove the oyster.

Note: If you are eating these as an appetizer, you won't need as many, but keep in mind, left over oysters will be great in stew or soup.

Serves 4–6

Carla

My friend Laurie Lewis and her husband, Peter, recently built a charming new home on Nantucket, and one of my favorite rooms is their very grand kitchen. Laurie is a very "at ease" cook, and when we arrive for dinner, she dons her apron, and we sit around her kitchen island and watch her cook a scrumptious meal. This is one of Laurie's favorite recipes, perfect to take up to Great Point on the Fourth of July. She suggests that you soak the bamboo skewers in a soda bottle filled to the top with water and the cap screwed on tightly. This way they will travel safely in the car and stay totally submerged until ready to use.

28–30 shrimps
1/2 cup olive oil
2 tablespoon rice wine vinegar
3 tablespoons Dijon mustard
1 tablespoon shallots, chopped
1 teaspoon fresh ginger, finely minced
2 cloves garlic, finely minced
1 tablespoon fresh dill, chopped
1 tablespoon fresh basil, chopped
Pinch of sugar

Clean and devein the shrimp first. (We use large shrimp.) Mix all the other ingredients together in a bowl and blend well with a whisk. Add the shrimp and toss several times to coat. Cover and refrigerate overnight or for several hours. Prepare the grill so that the coals are gray and not flaming. Thread the shrimp on the water soaked bamboo skewers and grill approximately 2 minutes per side, until they are firm and opaque but not dry. Be vigilant as they will cook quickly.

SWORDFISH MARINADE

This is a great marinade not only for swordfish but for any other seafood that you would like to marinate. The fresh ginger makes it particularly delicious.

3/4 cup teriyaki sauce
2/3 cup dry sherry
2 teaspoons minced
  garlic
2 teaspoons fresh ginger
1 teaspoon sesame oil

Combine all of the above ingredients and marinate the swordfish for 4–6 hours.

Serves 6

We saw a version of this recipe in our local paper and played with it a bit. The marinade is full of flavor and can be used as a basting sauce, then drizzled over the cooked salmon.

6 6-ounce salmon steaks
1 cup dry vermouth
1/4 cup fresh lemon juice
1/2 onion, finely chopped
2 garlic cloves, minced
2 teaspoons kosher salt
1/4 teaspoon fresh pepper
1/4 teaspoon thyme
2/3 cup melted butter

Put salmon steaks in Ziploc bag and cover with sauce. Marinate for 3 hours at room temperature. Put steaks on grill and brush with marinade. Grill for about 8 minutes per side. Drizzle with remaining marinade and serve.

SIDE DISHES

Blue Cheese Mash 145

Cheddar Chili Corn.. 146

Cheesy Creamy Spinach.. 149

Curried Rice 158

Green Beans and Garlic Packet 161

Grilled Asparagus 140

Grilled Corn 148

Grilled Potatoes with Blue Cheese 150

Grilled Tomatoes.. 154

Grilled Summer Vegetables 152

Marinated Mushroom Packet 161

Medley of Summer Vegetables Packet................. 162

Michael's Mushroom in Honor of Sydney 142

Pasta with Black Olive Pesto 144

Perfect Corn... 147

Potatoes Anna.. 151

Roasted Stuffed Peppers....................................... 163

Roy's Roasted Vidalias.. 153

Sesame Asparagus 141

Spanakopita Pie... 157

Stuffed Tomatoes 156

Sweet Potato Packet 160

Tex-Mex Rice.. 159

Tomato Spinach Pie... 155

Tomatoes and Shallots Packet 162

Serves 4

Sometimes you want a totally simple green vegetable with your marinated meat or fish. Asparagus works because it cooks up quickly on the grill and is easily dressed with a squeeze of lemon. We have added another asparagus dish that has a bit more punch but won't work as well if it is competing with the big flavor of a soy marinade like the Butterflied Leg of Lamb #2. Try both versions and decide for yourself.

1 bunch of asparagus
Olive oil
Lemon
Salt and pepper
Lemon zest

Trim asparagus and put in Ziploc bag. Pour in enough olive oil to coat lightly. When ready to eat, put asparagus on grill and turn gently with tongs after 3 or 4 minutes. When caramelized and cooked through, remove spears to a dish. Squeeze a few drops of olive oil and fresh lemon juice over spears, add salt and pepper, and garnish with lemon zest.

For a sensational twist on grilled asparagus, wrap each raw spear of asparagus with a slice of prosciutto and grill. When the prosciutto is browned and the spear is cooked through, arrange on a plate with a few drops of olive oil and a squeeze of lemon, and top with shaved parmigiano reggiano cheese.

Serves 4

This is a do-ahead side dish. It is a fresh take on asparagus that responds well to the citrus and the sesame. This one disappears, so make plenty if you have a crowd.

1 bunch asparagus
2 tablespoons sesame oil
1 tablespoon rice wine vinegar
1 tablespoon orange juice
Orange zest
Sesame seeds
Salt and pepper

Boil or steam asparagus and remove to platter. Add sesame oil and orange juice and vinegar. Add zest. Toast sesame seeds and sprinkle on. Season with salt and pepper.

Serves 4

Deborah

When my daughter Sydney was six years old, she ran into the kitchen proudly displaying what I thought was a soccer ball. Turned out it was a mushroom that was growing in our back yard. I had never seen a huge white round mushroom like it, but I immediately took it to Bill Maple at the Maria Mitchell House, where I learned it was a puffball. Once we determined it was safe and edible, I took it to Michael Shannon, a dear friend and the chef at the Club Car. By then, the *Inky Mirror* had showed up for a photo, and this mushroom became part of our family lore. Chef Michael whipped it into an appetizer that night on the menu for about a dozen lucky customers. We found another slightly smaller mushroom the next day, which we cooked ourselves. After that, we noticed the puffballs after a rain every summer in our yard on Vestal Street. Never again, however, did we have one that enormous.

When Michael Shannon gave me this amazing recipe, he told me that this sauce would work equally well on paillards of chicken, crabcakes, veal, or sole. If you are making it for fish, substitute fish stock for the chicken stock.

1 huge puffball mushroom, sliced into quarter-inch pieces
1/3 cup flour
3 eggs, beaten
2 tablespoons canola oil to coat pan
5 tablespoons sweet cream butter
1 tablespoon extra virgin olive oil
1 tablespoon shallots, chopped
1/4 cup champagne vinegar
1 cup white wine
1 1/2 cups chicken stock
1/4 cup lemon juice
3/4 cup heavy cream
1/2 cup diced, seeded tomatoes
1 scallion, chopped
1 tablespoon Dijon mustard
1 teaspoon chives, chopped
2 teaspoon tarragon, chopped

Dredge mushroom slices in flour and dip into beaten eggs. Pour canola oil into sauté pan and coat lightly. Turn heat to medium high. Lay dipped mushroom slices carefully in pan and sauté for about 30 seconds per side to brown. Season with salt and pepper. Turn slices to brown other side. Remove slices and lay on to paper towels. Lay another paper towel on top to soak off fat.

Wipe out the pan and add 1 tablespoon butter and 1 tablespoon olive oil. On medium-low heat, sweat the shallots for about 5 minutes. Do not brown. Add the champagne vinegar and the wine, turn up the heat, and reduce by half. Add the chicken stock and reduce by three quarters. Add lemon juice and heavy cream. Reduce until the sauce has a velvety body. Turn heat down and add the tomatoes and the scallion. Off heat, while sauce is still warm, whisk in the remaining 4 tablespoons of sweet butter. Whisk in the Dijon mustard. When that is done, add chopped fresh chives and tarragon.

Serves 6

Pesto is ubiquitous in the summer when none of us can get enough of fresh basil. This offers that taste but adds a very interesting twist. It is easily thrown together and will please everyone. It can be made in advance and served at room temperature, and it will feed many as a side dish.

1 pound linguini or pasta of choice
1/2 cup extra virgin olive oil
1 bunch fresh basil
3 cloves garlic
1 can black olives, pitted
1/2 cup pine nuts or chopped walnuts
4 ounces goat cheese
Salt and pepper

Cook pasta and drain. In a food processor, chop basil and olive oil. Add garlic and chop again. Add black olives and nuts and pulse until roughly chopped. Pour sauce on pasta and toss to incorporate. Crumble on goat cheese and season with salt and pepper. Toss again and serve.

Serves 6

Every now and then, we sacrifice sense for taste, and this one is worth it. It may not be a diet dish, but it is tasty and packed with flavor. The men will love this one, and if you are feeling a bit guilty, then at least you know that they had their spinach. And, of course, you can pare this down in terms of dressing and still have a delicious dish.

3 pounds potatoes, red or Yukon gold
Chili powder
Garlic powder
Salt and pepper
Vegetable oil
2 red onions, chopped
1 bag baby spinach
1 pound blue cheese
1/2 bottle favorite blue cheese dressing

Cut potatoes into chunks and put in water. Bring to a boil and simmer until they are fork tender. Add spices. Heat a cast-iron pan and add vegetable oil. Sauté onions until soft and add potatoes. Fry until crisp. Place spinach into pan, which will wilt the spinach and flavor the potatoes. Add blue cheese and blue cheese dressing. Season to taste.

Serves 8

This dish is so gooey and decadent that there is never a corn kernel left in the pot. Since it is preheated in the pot, covered in tin foil, and reheated on the grill, it is always welcome as one of the rare warm side dishes. You can't eat this one all the time, but if you have it once, you will most certainly want it again and again.

2 1-pound bags frozen corn
2 cans green chilies, chopped
8 ounces cream cheese
8 ounces cheddar cheese, shredded
2 tablespoons chili powder
2 tablespoons ground cumin
1/2 teaspoon jalapeno pepper powder or cayenne pepper
1 tablespoon garlic powder
Salt and pepper to taste

Combine all ingredients in a cast-iron skillet and warm over low heat until cheese is melted, stirring to prevent sticking. Cover with aluminum foil and set aside. Reheat on the grill until bubbling and serve with dinner.

Serves 6

Deborah

When I was talking with Julia Child about recipes some years back, we were discussing New England's finest produce. Locals believe there is no place on earth that produces better corn than the Northeast, and Julia was talking about ways to heighten the corn experience even further. "Fresh corn needs nothing," she said, "but a little cream and salt and pepper." Turns out, she was right. Butter, of course, will do instead of cream in this dish, but we are talking nirvana here. Also, fresh corn cooks very quickly, so taste as you go.

12 ears fresh corn
2/3 cup heavy cream
Salt and pepper

Cut the kernels from 12 ears of summer corn. Put them in a pan and pour on the cream. Stir and cook over medium heat for about 5 minutes. Taste the corn, and if it doesn't seem fully cooked, cook a bit longer. Season with salt and pepper.

Note: For a picnic, you can do all of this ahead, perhaps undercooking the corn by a minute or so. Rewarm over coals in a skillet and serve immediately.

Serves 12

Deborah

My neighbor Sharon Lappin is married to Harbormaster Ken Lappin. A Snow before she married, Sharon has spent much of her life on Nantucket and certainly done her share of cooking al fresco. She is never without tomatoes ripening on her windowsill and a wonderful pastry on her kitchen table being nibbled at by her kids and friends. She taught me the age-old method for grilling corn, and we have added a twist by using a secret sauce from another great friend, Pam Killen.

12 ears fresh corn
2 sticks butter, melted
Juice of three limes
Tabasco sauce or Belizian hot sauce
Salt

Peel husks back on corn but do not remove. Pull off all corn silk and return husks to corn. Soak corn in sea water. Melt butter and combine with lime juice and hot sauce. Pull corn from water and brush liberally with butter-lime combination. Grill on hot coals for about 20 minutes.

Serves 8

Everyone loves creamed spinach, and this recipe, which adds two of Italy's best cheeses, is especially popular. It's another dish that can be prepared in advance and kept warm. It won't suffer from being less than piping hot, but with the cheese, it must at least be warm when it is served.

Preheat oven to 400°

1 cup heavy cream
1/4 cup whole milk
1/2 teaspoon salt
1/2 teaspoon freshly ground black pepper
4 16-ounce packages frozen chopped spinach,
 thawed and squeezed dry
1 1/2 cups grated fontina cheese
2/3 cup freshly grated Parmigiano Reggiano cheese
1 onion, chopped

Stir the cream, milk, salt, and pepper in a medium-sized bowl. Add the spinach, fontina cheese, half the Parmigiano, and the onions. Mix well and turn the mixture into a gratin dish. Sprinkle remaining Parmigiano on top. Bake for 25 minutes.

Serves 6

Grilling sliced potatoes is simple and provides a smoky, crisp base to a sharp blue cheese dressing. Put the potatoes on before the meat and watch them to prevent burning. Once they are cooked, pour on the other ingredients while the potatoes are warm. This can sit at room temperature as it only gets better as it soaks up the different flavors. The next day, if you have leftovers, fry them up in a cast-iron skillet until they crisp up again.

3 Idaho baking potatoes
1/2 cup olive oil
1/2 cup red wine vinegar
4 ounces crumbled blue cheese
2 scallions, chopped, including green part
Salt and pepper

Slice potatoes into 1/4" thin pieces. Put slices on grill and turn with tongs when they have grill marks on them and begin to brown. Remove when the other side looks cooked. Immediately pour on oil and vinegar and add blue cheese. Stir so that the cheese begins to melt. Add scallions and season to taste. Stir and serve.

Serves 6 · 8

This is a pretty famous dish, and everyone has his or her own take on it. We love to intersperse the layers with plenty of chopped garlic and season each layer. When you flip the potatoes, garnish the crispy top layer with chopped fresh chives. This dish must be made in a cast-iron pan; it can be transported to the beach and kept warm, but it might lose some crispness. Our suggestion is to roast it at home for 35 minutes, cover it with foil, take it to the beach in a cast-iron pan, and finish it on the grill for another 10–15 minutes. Turn it onto a dish and, voila, you will have a dish so gorgeous and browned and crisp that every morsel will be devoured.

Preheat oven to 400°

4 baking potatoes
1 stick of butter
4 cloves fresh garlic, chopped
Salt and pepper
Chives, chopped

Peel the potatoes and slice them very thinly. A mandolin will do the best job as you want them no thicker than 1/4 inch. Layer the potatoes into a cast-iron skillet, beginning in the middle with a rose-petal pattern. Continue layering them in a circle, taking them all the way to the outer edge. Drizzle butter over the first layer, sprinkle on the garlic, and generously season with salt and pepper. Repeat until you have used up your potatoes. Cover and bake in the oven for a total of about 45–50 minutes. If you are taking these with you, follow the directions above. When the potatoes are finished, take two pot holders and hold an inverted plate over the pan. Grabbing the whole thing together, flip the potatoes onto the plate. Your potatoes should be golden and crisp. Garnish with chives and serve in pie-shaped wedges.

Serves 10

This dish changes according to whim, requiring only a grilling basket and your choice of farm-fresh veggies. We usually include the little red potatoes and vary the rest. This is a good sampling and works for a crowd.

10 new potatoes, halved
1 small eggplant, sliced thinly and salted
2 zucchinis, sliced lengthwise
1 summer squash, sliced lengthwise
1 red pepper, sliced into 1-inch wedges
1 red onion, cut into 8 applelike wedges
1/2 cup extra virgin olive oil
1/3 cup balsamic vinegar
2 cloves garlic, minced
Salt and pepper
Basil leaves, chopped

Lay all vegetables out in basket, adding the eggplant after it has had 15 minutes to salt. (You can grill the eggplant separately if you want as it is easy to retrieve from the grill with tongs.) Place basket over coals and cook for about 7 minutes per side. Pour cooked vegetables into a serving dish and sprinkle with olive oil and balsamic vinegar, minced garlic, and salt and pepper. Garnish with chopped basil.

ROY'S ROASTED VIDALIAS

Serves 4

Deborah

Every once in a while, we are fortunate to meet someone who tickles and delights us. Roy Bailey was such a person. I met him first at one of Jimmy Barker's artists' luncheons, when I sat next to him. I wasn't there for 5 minutes before he had me laughing so hard my stomach hurt. Roy had this effect on everyone, as witnessed by the constant stream of people who trickled into his studio to hear his latest tale or joke. He made everyone's day better. My children loved him, my mother and father loved him, my ex-husband loved him, and my new boyfriend loved him. To my delight, he moved across the street from my Vestal Street house. He became one of my best friends. For the 10 years I was lucky enough to have Roy Bailey as my across-the-street neighbor, I not only laughed well but ate well. Roy was a natural cook, throwing the simplest ingredients together to make a surprise treat. Whenever he grilled a steak, he threw these onions onto the coals. They were amazing and have become part of our regular repertoire.

**2 vidalia onions, cut into
  4 wedges each
2 ounces butter
1/2 cup balsamic vinegar
Salt and pepper**

Place all ingredients on a sheet of aluminum foil and fold into a packet. Put directly onto gray coals and cook for 20 minutes.

Serves 6

Here is a great way to enjoy summer's bounty. Plum tomatoes on the grill are quick, lend themselves well to caramelization, and are a compliment to almost any grilled meat or fish. Do watch these tomatoes closely, though, as they take less than 10 minutes to cook.

1 pound plum tomatoes
Extra virgin olive oil
Balsamic vinegar
Salt and pepper
Fresh basil, optional

Cut tomatoes in half lengthwise and season with salt and pepper. Place cut side down on hot grill and cook for a couple of minutes. Use tongs to handle them so they do not break apart. They will be charred when you turn them over. Cook for another few minutes and place on a platter. Drizzle with olive oil and balsamic vinegar. Season again.

Note: If you take a 16 ounce bottle of balsamic vinegar add a half cup of sugar and reduce it on the stove by half, you will end up with a wonderful concentrated "gastrique". A few drops will go a long way. It will be useful on other things as well, for instance, drizzled onto grilled chicken or zucchini. Great to keep around.

Serves 6

Here is another side dish that sparkles with fresh tomatoes and spinach, a classic combination. The cheese and eggs make it more substantial and give it a satisfying twist. Easy to make in advance and transport, this works as a main course at lunch with a salad and should please the vegetarians. At dinner, it is a great alternative to potatoes or pasta.

Preheat oven to 400°

2 cups ricotta cheese
5 eggs
1 cup light sour cream
4 ounces crumbled goat cheese
1/2 stick butter
4 ounces grated Parmesan cheese
3 cloves garlic
1 pint cherry tomatoes
Salt and pepper
2 boxes frozen spinach

Soften ricotta cheese by beating in a Mixmaster. Beat eggs and add to cheese. Add sour cream and crumbled goat cheese and blend. Melt butter in bottom of baking dish and dust with half the Parmesan cheese. Chop garlic and toss with halved tomatoes. Season with salt and pepper and bake for 15 minutes. Put frozen spinach in microwave and heat for 5 minutes. Squeeze out all moisture and spread throughout tomato and garlic dish. Pour cheese mixture on top. Sprinkle with remaining Parmesan and bake until set, about 20 minutes. Serve warm or at room temperature.

Serves 6

This is a nice recipe for a fall picnic when there are lots of wonderful tomatoes from the summer vines. The cornbread-stuffed tomatoes go nicely with burgers, chicken, or fish and serve as a great side dish or even as a main dish.

6 ripe tomatoes
3 cups crumbled cornbread
3/4 cup mayonnaise
6 slices bacon, cooked and crumbled
3 green onions, chopped
Salt and pepper to taste

Remove the cores and pulp from the tomatoes and put them in a bowl. Be careful not to tear the shells while doing this. Mix together the tomato pulp, cornbread, and remaining five ingredients. Spoon this mixture into the shells and wrap each shell in heavy-duty aluminum foil and place on a grill with gray coals that are not flaming. Heat the tomatoes for approximately 8–10 minutes.

Serves 12

This is an easier take on the tiny spinach pies that became popular on the hors d'oeuvres circuit about 10 years back. The dish is an obvious casserole with as much flavor and as many do-ahead options as individual pies, with half the fuss. If you make this ahead, rewarm it in a low-temp oven and keep it covered in foil. This recipe is from an all-time favorite cookbook by Marion Morash. Morash, who was once the executive chef at the Straight Wharf Restaurant, and who's husband produced Julia Child's cooking show, wrote, to our mind, the definitive vegetable cookbook, *The Victory Garden Cookbook*, published nearly 25 years ago. It is timeless and our vegetable bible.

Preheat oven to 375°

7 cups blanched spinach
2 onions, chopped
2 sticks salted butter
6 large eggs, beaten
2 pounds ricotta or cottage cheese
1 pound feta cheese, crumbled
Salt and pepper
1/2 pound frozen filo dough (available in the frozen section of your market)

Chop spinach. Melt two tablespoons butter in a large frying pan and sauté onions until soft. Add chopped spinach. Turn up heat and cook until moisture is gone. Remove from heat. Melt remaining butter in separate pan. In a bowl, mix cheeses into beaten eggs and add the spinach and onions. Season with salt and pepper. Butter a lasagna pan or baking dish and spread the spinach and cheese mixture into bottom of pan. Begin layering filo sheets one at a time, painting each sheet with melted butter. Continue layering until you have about 10 sheets of filo dough. Bake in a preheated oven for 15 minutes and then lower temperature to 350°. Bake for another 30 minutes, covering filo with foil if it gets too dark. Let rest before cutting.

Serves 10

This is a rice dish that works well at room temperature. It has a savory taste, which you may choose to accent with raisins. As is, it is quite different and very delicious.

3 cups long-grain or basmati rice
Water
2 large jars artichoke hearts
1 bunch scallions, chopped
1 jar green olives, chopped
1 1/2 green pepper, chopped
3 tablespoons curry powder
1 1/3 cup light mayonnaise

Boil rice according to package instructions. Add all other ingredients and stir.

Serves 6

Everyone loves Tex-Mex, and this rice dish offers Southwestern flavor and plenty of punch. It is another one of those dishes that can be prepared and kept warm, but it also tastes good at room temperature. Once you have made it, you can play with the amounts and the seasonings and make enough for a crowd. This makes a great side to grilled chicken.

2 cups long-grain rice
4 cups water
2 tablespoons olive oil
1 onion, chopped
1–2 jalapeno peppers, chopped
1 tomato, seeded and chopped
1 cup Monterey Jack or cheddar cheese, shredded
1 teaspoon chili powder
1 teaspoon cumin seed
1 cup sour cream
Salt and pepper
Cilantro for garnish

Cook rice on stove top. In separate pan, sauté onion in olive oil, adding pepper and tomato once the onion has softened. Add rice to ingredients and stir to incorporate. Add cheddar while rice is hot, allowing it to melt as you stir it in.

Add spices and sour cream, and salt and pepper to taste. Serve with chopped cilantro.

Serves 2

Deborah

My daughter, Michaele, is a vegetarian who does not like having her food cooked on a meat-encrusted grill, and she devised this nifty way of having her meals prepared alongside everyone's steak or burgers. It has worked so well, we do it ourselves all the time for side dishes. Her first attempt at this was a sweet potato dish, classic, utterly simple, and an improvement over the oven version.

1 yam or sweet potato, peeled and diced
3 large marshmallows

Put ingredients on a sheet of aluminum foil and fold into a packet. Put on grill and cook for 15 minutes. Beware of steam when opening up. Slide onto plate and eat.

GREEN BEANS AND GARLIC

12 ounces green beans, trimmed
6 garlic cloves, unpeeled
1 tablespoon cooking oil
1 tablespoon water
1 teaspoon lemon juice
1 jalapeno pepper, cut into thin strips

Combine all of the above ingredients in a bowl and then place the bean mixture in a large packet of heavy-duty aluminum foil. Place the packet on the grill over medium coals and grill for 20 minutes, turning once. Remove packet from grill and let cool slightly. Open the packet and place back on the grill and continue grilling for 5 minutes more, or until crisp and tender.

MARINATED MUSHROOMS

Serves 2 as a main dish, serves 4 as a side

In the case of this and any other dish with marinade, you should transport it separately and assemble at the picnic to guard against leakage.

1 pound mushrooms, sliced
2 tablespoons olive oil
1 tablespoon fresh lemon juice
1 clove garlic, chopped
Salt and pepper

Place all ingredients in foil, and fold into a packet. Put on grill for 15 minutes.

MEDLEY OF SUMMER VEGETABLES

Serves 4

**1 zucchini
1 tomato
1 red onion
1 summer squash
1 clove garlic, chopped**

Slice all vegetables and sprinkle with olive oil, and salt and pepper. Fold into packet and cook for 12 minutes.

TOMATOES AND SHALLOTS

Serves 2

**1 ripe summer tomato
3 shallots, sliced
Extra virgin olive oil
Salt and pepper**

Slice tomatoes and cover with sliced shallots. Sprinkle with extra virgin olive oil and salt and pepper. Fold into packets. Put on grill for 12 minutes.

Serves 6

This is another one of Nancy Verde Barr Bailey's most popular recipes. The many distinctive flavors in the recipe highlight southern Italian cooking - colorful, fragrant, and delectable. This dish can be made ahead and served at room temperature.

Preheat oven to 350°

3 red peppers
3 yellow peppers
2 tablespoons raisins
1 cup breadcrumbs (Panko or French bread)
1/4 cup brined black olives, pitted and chopped
3 tablespoons toasted pine nuts
3 tablespoons fresh basil, chopped
3 tablespoons Italian parsley, chopped
2 tablespoons capers, drained and chopped
2 garlic cloves, minced
2 anchovy filets, minced
1/2 teaspoon salt
5 tablespoons olive oil

Lightly oil a baking dish. Char peppers over flame or broiler and put into bag and close. Blacken all sides but do not soften. Let stand 10 minutes. Rinse and peel peppers under cold water. Cut lengthwise in half and scrape out stems and seeds. Arrange peppers cut side up in single layer in baking dish.

Place raisins in bowl and cover with hot water; let stand for 10 minutes. Drain and chop. Place in medium-sized bowl and add next eight ingredients. Toss to combine. Season with salt and pepper. Add 3 tablespoons olive oil and combine. Spoon ingredients into pepper shells and drizzle 2 tablespoons olive oil over peppers. Bake 30 minutes.

Beach Blanket Espresso Brownies 166

Brant Point Butterscotch Thins 180

Bridesmaids' Biscuits 182

Daffodil Weekend Cake 168

Fourth of July Blueberry Pie 171

Fourth of July Firecracker Cakes.. 172

Grilled Peaches 174

Ice Cream Sandwiches 175

Mascarpone and Meringues 167

Nantucket Blues.. 181

Orange Raspberry Ambrosia 177

Pink Lemonade Cookies 185

Rosemary Shortbread Cookies... 186

S'mores Cake 179

Summer Plum Blueberry Nectarine Cobbler.................... 176

Texas Gold Bars.. 187

Watermelon Cake 188

Makes 18 brownies

Brownies have been around since they were first introduced as a recipe in an 1897 Sears catalogue. Since then, they have been baked in many versions, and we love this one by Susan Ward. She was the local food critic for the *Inky Mirror* for many years. Her own food is as good as that at most of the places she has reviewed, and this recipe for her brownies is proof. Whenever she asks what she can bring to the picnic, we always ask for these gooey delicious treats.

Preheat oven to 350°

6 ounces semisweet chocolate
2 teaspoons espresso powder or instant coffee granules
8 tablespoons unsalted butter, at room temperature
1 teaspoon vanilla
2 eggs, slightly beaten
3/4 cup sugar
1/2 cup flour
Pinch of salt

Butter and flour an 8-inch square pan. Melt chocolate in double boiler. Add espresso powder and stir well. Remove pan from heat and add butter. Beat until smooth. Stir in vanilla and eggs. Sift together sugar, salt, and flour. Add to chocolate mixture. Blend thoroughly. Bake for 30 minutes.

Serves 6

This is another simple dessert, made in minutes, easily transported, and totally rewarding. The smooth cream, coupled with the crunch of the meringues, makes it an interesting taste treat—indeed, this one is a way to give your mouth a party.

2 pints fresh berries—your choice of raspberries, blackberries, strawberries, blueberries, or any combination thereof
1/4 cup sugar
1 cup mascarpone cheese
1 cup whipping cream
12 meringue cookies

Wash berries and drain. Sprinkle on sugar and stir. Rest. Put mascarpone cheese in bowl and bring to room temperature. Whip heavy cream and fold gently into cheese. Chill. Bring each thing to the beach in a separate container. When ready, crumble meringue cookie into cup and top with berries and cream. Sprinkle a bit more cookie on top. Serve.

Serves 8–10

Carla

One of my childhood memories is of my grandmother arriving at our Rhode Island home in the spring with a cake carrier filled with a homemade cake she called a daffodil cake because when you cut into it, the center is white and yellow. My grandmother was a great old-fashioned cook, and I feel fortunate to have some of her recipes. It is the perfect cake to celebrate with on Daffodil Weekend, and I wanted it to fit in with all the daffodil-themed decorations, so I took a course on making edible daffodils to accent my frosting. If that is too much, however, it is possible to find already-made daffodil-cake decorations in some specialty stores.

Preheat oven to 350°

Cake
3/4 cup sifted flour
3/4 cup egg whites
1/4 teaspoon salt
3/4 teaspoon cream of tartar
1 cup sifted sugar
1/4 teaspoon almond extract
3 egg yolks, well beaten
1 1/2 tablespoons sugar

Icing
1 cup solid shortening
4 cups confectioner's sugar
1 teaspoon vanilla extract
1 tablespoon meringue powder
4–5 tablespoons water

Sift flour four times. Beat egg whites and salt until foamy and add cream of tartar. Continue beating until stiff but not dry. Fold in 1 cup of sugar slowly. Sift flour over mixture in small amounts, folding carefully. Divide into two parts. Add almond extract to one, and into the other half add the egg yolks beaten thick with the additional 1 1/2 tablespoons of sugar. Drop by tablespoons into an ungreased tube pan, alternating mixtures. Bake for 45–60 minutes. Remove from oven and invert the pan to cool.

Beat all icing ingredients together on high speed until you have the desired spreading consistency. Frost cake when it is totally cool. Decorate with edible daffodils.

Serves 8

With strawberries and blueberries proliferating during the summer months, it is a snap to look patriotic on the Fourth of July. We love this recipe from Ruth Barney because of its festive appearance and its fabulous flavor. Naturally, we use Nantucket blueberries, which we search out each year at top-secret locations. This is not only patriotic but Nantucket chauvinistic.

Preheat oven to 425°

1/2 cup oil
2 tablespoons milk
1 1/2 cups flour
1/2 teaspoon salt
1 1/2 teaspoons sugar
2 pints blueberries
1 cup sugar
1 tablespoon cornstarch
1 1/2 tablespoons lemon juice
1/2 stick butter
1/2 cup flour
1/2 cup sugar
1 teaspoon cinnamon
Blueberries and strawberries (for decorating)

Combine the first five ingredients in a bowl, kneading well with your hands, then press the dough into the pie plate for the crust.

Combine the blueberries, sugar, cornstarch, and lemon juice in a bowl and pour into the pie crust.

Combine the last four ingredients to make a crumbly topping and then put on top of the blueberry mixture.

Bake the pie for 10 minutes, then lower the heat to 350° and back for another 35 minutes. Decorate the top with fresh strawberries and blueberries.

Serves 6–8

Carla

The Fourth of July is celebrated in grand style on Nantucket, and these cakes made to look like sparklers will really add to your patriotic picnic. My son's birthday is near the Fourth, and one year, instead of making my traditional American flag cake, I made these sparklers in small sizes so that everyone could have one. It was quite a hit, but this recipe calls for a bit of planning ahead. I use my Victoria Sponge Jelly Roll recipe from England for the cake part, so they are not only fun to look at but very tasty too.

Preheat oven to 350°

3 eggs
2 tablespoons sour cream
3/4 cup sugar
4 tablespoons butter, melted
1 tablespoon lemon juice
1 cup flour
1 teaspoon baking powder
1/4 teaspoon salt
2 cups raspberry preserves

Icing
1 cup butter
4 cups confectioner's sugar
1 teaspoon clear vanilla extract
1 tablespoon meringue powder
4–5 tablespoons water

Beat eggs and sour cream in a medium-sized bowl. Add sugar and beat until well mixed and stiff. Beat in the butter and the lemon juice. In a separate bowl, sift the flour, baking powder, and salt together. Gently fold the flour mixture into the butter mixture. Spread the mixture into a 11" × 17" jelly roll pan that has been greased and lined with parchment paper.

Bake for 15 minutes. Remove from oven and cool on a cake rack. Flip the pan over onto a dish towel and remove the parchment paper. Spread the raspberry preserves on the cake and roll up from the long side. Cut the jelly roll into the sizes you want for your sparklers and frost with homemade icing.

Mix shortening and extract together until creamy smooth. Add confectioner's sugar, meringue powder, and water and beat with hand mixer until fully blended. Divide the icing into thirds, leaving one-third white, tinting one-third with red gel food coloring, and tinting the last third with blue gel food coloring.

Frost some of the sparkler cakes white, some red, and some blue. Decorate with stars and stripes. To make stars on the sparkler, you will need a pastry bag and pastry tip #16, and to make stripes you will need pastry tip #3. Use either the leftover white, red, or blue frosting. Stick American flags on toothpicks into the top of the sparklers.

Serves 4

When peaches are finally available, we can't get enough of them. We use them to make peach ice cream, and in cobblers, and at breakfast with heavy cream. But they also make a great dessert at a beach picnic. They are utterly simple to prepare, and they remind us of summer's fleeting glory.

4 firm but ripe peaches
1/2 cup sugar
Heavy whipping cream

Split peaches and remove stones. Sprinkle peaches with sugar and let stand for 5 minutes. Place peaches on grill sugar side up and cook for about 4 minutes. Turn to put sugar side down. Remove peaches and serve with a dollop of whipped cream, or you can simply drizzle on the heavy cream.

The only trick here is getting the ice cream to the beach. In the best of circumstances, it will have softened somewhat, which makes assembly of these variety treats easy. The best store-bought cookies for this dessert are Pepperidge Farm sugar cookies and Nabisco chocolate wafers, but you can pick your own personal favorites and mix and match. The possibilities are limited only by your imagination.

Sugar Cookies and Sorbets
Mango Sorbet
Black raspberry Sorbet
Orange Sorbet

Chocolate Wafers and Ice Cream
Chocolate Ice Cream
Vanilla Ice Cream
Mint chocolate chip Ice Cream

Put softened ice cream between two cookies and press to form a sandwich.

This is a fail-proof dessert that can be used with any combination of fruit that you like. Blackberries are a great substitute for the blueberries, and peaches for the nectarines. If the fruit you choose is tart, toss it in sugar before you cook.

Preheat oven to 400°

5 nectarines
5 plums
1 pint blueberries
1 cup flour
1 cup sugar
1 egg
1 stick butter

Cut up fruit and put in bottom of heavy baking dish. Combine flour and sugar, and add egg. Add softened butter and mix well. Spread dough over fruit and bake for 40 minutes or until top is browned. Serve while warm with ice cream or whipped cream.

Serves 6

This is a light and heavenly way to end a meal. It is completely healthy, and the coconut takes the simple blend of fruits to a whole new level. This is one you will serve at winter dinner parties as well, satisfying all the women who are watching their weight and the men who long for a sweet finale.

**6 Valencia oranges, peeled and broken into sections,
   all membranes removed
2 pints raspberries
1 10-ounce bag of sweetened coconut flakes, toasted**

Layer one-third of the orange sections into the bottom of a glass bowl. Follow with one-third of the raspberries. Top with the toasted coconut. Repeat in two more layers. It will look colorful and beautiful, and when you serve it, the hint of coconut will pervade the fruit and make for a perfect combination.

Serves 16

When our kids were young, no beach picnic was complete without s'mores, that gooey concoction created by the Girl Scouts in 1927. The original S'mores recipe called for toasting "two marshmallows to a crisp, gooey state, and putting them into a graham cracker and chocolate bar sandwich." Needless to say, one of the big attractions for the kids was sitting around the fire watching their marshmallows bubble on the stick. The young folk love the mess of it, and everyone loves the taste. Once our children got older, we recreated the flavor without the mess in a gooey, crunchy cake. This is our version of adult s'mores.

Preheat oven to 350°

1 cup all-purpose flour
1 1/2 cups graham cracker crumbs
1 teaspoon baking powder
1/2 teaspoon baking soda
1/2 teaspoon salt
1 cup firmly packed brown sugar
1/2 cup shortening
3 eggs
1 cup milk
1 cup miniature semisweet chocolate chips
7 ounces of marshmallow cream.

Grease and flour 13" × 9" pan. In medium-sized bowl, combine flour, graham cracker crumbs, baking powder, baking soda, and salt and mix well.

In large bowl, beat brown sugar, eggs, and shortening until well blended. Add flour mixture and milk, and mix at low speed until well blended. Then, beat 1 minute at medium speed. Stir in 2/3 cup of the chocolate chips and spread batter evenly in the pan.

Bake for 25 minutes. Cool for 15 minutes.

In a small saucepan, melt remaining 1/3 cup chocolate chips over low heat. Spoon marshmallow cream on top of the warm cake and carefully spread with a knife. Then, drizzle with the melted chocolate, swirling through the marshmallow cream. Cool completely before cutting into serving pieces.

Makes 30 cookies

Carla

One night, a group of friends decided to meet at Brant Point for dessert and coffee. What fun we had sitting by the lighthouse watching all the boating activities as nightfall crept in. We brought a big thermos of hot chocolate for the children who loved the evening. This recipe was my contribution to the sweets table. It came from my grandmother, who always loved anything with butterscotch. When I was little, we used to sit on her front porch and indulge in coffee ice cream and butterscotch thins—what a great memory that is for me. Since they were such a hit at our dessert picnic on the point, I named them Brant Point Butterscotch Thins, and here's to you, Nana, for always being such a big part of my life.

Preheat oven to 375°

1 cup butterscotch chips
1 stick unsalted butter
1 1/2 cups all-purpose flour
3/4 teaspoon baking soda
2/3 cup dark brown sugar, firmly packed
1 large egg
1 teaspoon vanilla
1/3 cup pecans, chopped finely

Melt butterscotch chips in a double boiler with the butter, stirring. In a bowl, whisk together flour and baking soda. In another bowl, with an electric mixer, beat together butterscotch mixture, sugar, egg, and vanilla. Add flour mixture in batches and stir in pecans.

On a sheet of wax paper, form the dough into an 8-inch log, using the wax paper as a guide. Twist the ends of the wax paper to enclose the log, then freeze it, tightly wrapped in foil, for at least 1 hour or until ready to use.

Remove log from freezer and let stand until it can be cut, about 2 minutes. Cut log with a sharp knife into 1/4-inch slices and arrange slices at least 3 inches apart on baking sheets. Let slices come to room temperature and bake in batches in middle of oven until thin and no longer puffed, about 8 minutes. Cool cookies before removing them from the cookie sheets.

Makes 3 dozen

Carla

My daughter and her friends have always enjoyed getting together at our house for a cookie-making party, whether it be at Christmas or Easter or for a picnic by the seaside. It always amazes me how creative the girls are with the decorating of the cookies. We, of course, had to create a Nantucket cookie, and this is what we came up with.

Preheat oven to 400°

1 cup butter, softened
1 cup sugar
1 egg
1 teaspoon vanilla
2 1/2 cups all-purpose flour
1 teaspoon baking powder

Glaze
5 cups powdered sugar
1/4 cup water
2 tablespoons butter, softened
Blue food coloring
Colored sugar crystals (sanding sugar)

Combine the 1 cup of butter, sugar, egg, and vanilla in a mixing bowl. Beat at medium speed until creamy, approximately 2–3 minutes. Reduce speed to low, and add flour and baking powder. Beat until well mixed.

Divide dough into thirds and shape each third into a ball. Wrap in wax paper, flatten, and chill until firm, about 1 hour.

Roll out dough on a lightly floured surface, one-third at a time. The dough should be 1/8-inch thick. Cut out the cookies with a fish-shaped cookie cutter and place 1 inch apart on ungreased cookie sheets. Bake for 6–10 minutes or until lightly browned. Cool completely.

Combine powdered sugar, water, and 2 tablespoons butter in a bowl and beat at medium speed, adding extra water if necessary. Tint with the blue food coloring and glaze the cookies. Add sanding sugars or sprinkles if desired.

Makes 3 dozen

Carla

This is a very traditional cookie recipe but always a hit. I made it for a bridesmaids' luncheon that I gave for a friend's daughter. It was a lovely day, and all the girls were merry and giggly. These cookies are especially nice served with a cup of peppermint tea. So easy and so yummy!

Preheat oven to 350°

1 cup butter, softened
1/2 cup powdered sugar
1 teaspoon vanilla
2 cups flour, sifted
1/2 teaspoon salt
1 cup pecans, chopped

Mix all of the ingredients together and roll into small balls. Then, roll in extra powdered sugar and bake on an ungreased baking sheet for 10 minutes, or until golden.

Makes 4 dozen

When our children were young, one of their favorite things to do was to set up a lemonade stand, particularly down by the pond in Quidnet. They would make up lemonade and packaged brownie mixes, but the customers seemed to love the Pink Lemonade Cookies the best. This recipe was originally for a lemon cookie—we added a little red food coloring to make them pink.

Preheat oven to 400°

1 cup sugar
1/4 cup butter, softened
1 egg
2 teaspoon grated lemon peel
1 teaspoon lemon juice
1–2 drops red food coloring
1 cup flour
1/4 teaspoon salt
1/2 teaspoon baking powder
Powdered sugar (optional)

Combine sugar, butter, egg, lemon peel, lemon juice, and red food coloring in a large bowl. Beat at medium speed until creamy, about 2 minutes. Reduce the speed to low and add flour, salt, and baking powder. Beat until well mixed. Cover with Saran Wrap and chill until firm, at least 1 hour.

Remove from refrigerator, shape dough into small balls, and roll in remaining sugar. Place on greased cookie sheet and flatten balls with the bottom of a glass dipped in sugar. Bake for approximately 5–7 minutes. Cool, and sprinkle cookies with powdered sugar, if desired.

Makes 2 dozen

Carla

This recipe is perfect for teatime or maybe a bridal celebration at the beach. The cookies can be made as small as you like, which is what most people seem to prefer. I serve these in my shop on Christmas Stroll weekend with my Hot Cranberry Punch. The fragrance of the rosemary lends sophistication and lifts a classic cookie to a new level.

Preheat oven to 350°

8 tablespoons butter
1/4 cup superfine sugar
1 1/2 cups all-purpose flour
2 teaspoons fresh rosemary, finely chopped
2 tablespoons colored sugar for sprinkling (optional)

Cream butter and sugar until smooth. Work in the flour and rosemary to make a soft dough, then shape into a ball. Roll out the dough on a floured surface to about 1/4-inch thick, and cut out rounds to whatever size you like. For a bridal party, you may want to cut them into small hearts.

Bake on a greased baking sheet for 15–20 minutes or until shortbread begins to change color. Cool the cookies on a wire rack and then sprinkle with the colored sugar.

Makes 48 bars

Our friend Mary Jo Beck has made these wonderful bars for many years on Nantucket and has become quite famous for them. As with so many recipes, the origin is colorful. Twenty years ago, Mary Jo got this one off her Houston electric bill. She has been asked for them so often she now knows that when a beach picnic is in the works, she has to start baking. They are sweet and good and always enjoyed by all. Thank you, MJB, and your electric company for sharing your Texas recipe with us and our cookbook.

Preheat oven to 325°

1 package yellow cake mix
1 egg, lightly beaten
1/2 cup margarine, melted
1 teaspoon vanilla
8 ounces cream cheese
1 pound powdered sugar
2 eggs, lightly beaten

Combine cake mix, egg, and melted margarine. Press into ungreased 9" × 13" Pyrex pan (not metal). Mix remaining ingredients and spread over top. Bake for 50 minutes. Cool before cutting.

Serves 10–12

Carla

This is definitely a perfect beach picnic cake as it looks just like a watermelon when it is all decorated. I have simplified this recipe in many ways, such as using prepared frosting instead of making a homemade buttercream. It usually happens that I get so busy with my shop in the summer that I need some easy, fun recipes to fall back on. You will love the way it looks.

Preheat oven to 350°

1 package strawberry cake mix
1 3-ounce package watermelon gelatin
2 eggs
1 1/4 cups water
1/4 cup vegetable oil
2 1/2 cups prepared vanilla frosting
Red and green food coloring
Chocolate chips

Combine cake mix, gelatin, eggs, water, and oil and beat on low speed until moistened. Then, beat on high until well blended. Grease and flour two 9-inch round pans and pour the mixture in. Bake for 35 minutes. Cool for 10 minutes, then remove cakes to rack to cool further.

Put 1 1/4 cups frosting in a bowl and tint red. Tint remaining 1 1/8 cup frosting green, and leave last 1/8 of the frosting white. Place one cake layer on a plate and spread the top with some of the red frosting, then top with the second layer. Frost the top of the cake with the remaining red frosting, leaving 3/4 inch around the edge. Frost sides and top edge with green frosting. With a pastry bag filled with white frosting, pipe around edge where green and red frosting meet.

For seeds, you can insert chocolate chips upside down into the cake top.

COCKTAILS

Bloody Mary 193

Blue Moon 192

Bring on the Baby Cocktail 194

Caipirinha 195

Cisco-Tini 197

Goombay Smash 198

Hot Buttered Rum 199

Madaket Mojito... 192

Madequecham Margarita................................... 200

Mango and Malibu 201

Moscow Mule 201

Nantucket Iced Tea... 202

Nantucket Planter's Punch 201

Pina Colada 202

Raspberry Wine Punch 205

Royal Raspberry Punch 206

Sundown Cooler.. 208

Warm Cranberry Punch.................................... 209

Whiskey Punch 206

White Wine Lemonade 207

BLUE MOON

We started making this drink because we loved the name. This gorgeous tropical concoction wows them every time, and it manages to taste as good as it looks.

1 measure blue curaçao liqueur
1 measure golden rum, like Mount Gay
1/3 measure lemonade
2/3 measure fresh pineapple juice

Mix all ingredients together and shake. Pour over ice in a highball glass. Garnish with a slice of fresh pineapple.

MADAKET MOJITO

Seems like the world discovered Mojitos a few years ago, and now, because of their refreshing mint and lime flavor, they are de rigueur at our parties. We have tried lots of variations, and needless to say, this is our favorite. We offer a recipe here which you can tailor to your own palate.

1 lime
1–2 tablespoons sugar (according to your palate)
8 mint leaves
2–4 ounces club soda
2 ounces white rum
Ice

Cut the lime in slices and put in the bottom of a glass. Add the sugar to taste and all the mint. Press on the lime mixture with a pestle or a spoon until the lime releases its oils, and the sugar and mint are broken down and incorporated. Add ice and club soda to two-thirds full. Top with white rum. Garnish with mint sprig.

BLOODY MARY

Deborah

Everyone has his or her own version of this popular cocktail. We have been drinking them this way since we were novices and our dear friend made up his version. We approached our drinks like dinner entrees, trying lots of twists and tweaks to perfect the finished product. George Hibbard proudly offered this drink to all his friends. Sadly, he has long since died, but his cocktail is immortal, and we know he would be thrilled about that.

1 measure Absolut vodka
1 teaspoon ketchup
1 teaspoon Worcestershire sauce
1/2 teaspoon Lawry's Seasoned Salt
1/2 teaspoon celery flakes
3 measures Clamato juice
Lemon wedges and celery sticks

Mix first six ingredients and shake well. Pour over ice cubes, and squeeze in the juice of one lemon wedge. Garnish with second wedge or celery stick.

BRING ON THE BABY COCKTAIL

Deborah

When I was nine months pregnant with a baby that had kept me in bed for three months, my mother came to await the birth. Three weeks later, my mother was still there (waiting, watching, asking) for that baby's arrival. On the twenty-third day of her vigil, I finally succumbed to a cocktail. My mother whipped up a drink she remembered from her Easton Street days - of gin and lime and mint. It was a hot day, I was completely tense, and the drink equaled relief. My mother and husband and I had the drinks and started laughing. I laughed so hard my water broke and finally my daughter Chase was born. I paid the price when I learned that alcohol slows down labor, but I remember how delicious that drink was, and we have made it many times. I never have it without remembering its history.

2 measures gin
1 1/2 measures fresh lime juice
3/4 measure simple syrup
8 leaves fresh mint, chopped fine
Crushed ice

Put first four ingredients into blender and pour over crushed ice.

CAIPIRINHA

This Brazilian cocktail is now all the rage here in America. With the lime and sugar, it is utterly refreshing and very simple to make. For the authentic version, it is essential that you use cachaça rum, which is made from sugar cane and is distinctive in taste from other rums. Also, muddle your lime and sugar just enough to bring out the oil in the limes and enhance the flavor; muddling for too long makes the drink bitter. If you can't find cachaça, try this method with vodka. If you use white rum instead, the drink is called a Caipirissima.

1 lime, quartered
Sugar to taste
2 ounces cachaça rum
Crushed ice

Put three of the lime quarters pulp side up in the bottom of highball glass and add sugar. Muddle with a spoon or pestle to break down pulp and incorporate sugar. Add rum and ice. Top with last quarter of lime.

CISCO BREWERY is one of those marvelous Nantucket places that offer a fun afternoon tour. Cisco Brewers is actually only one of three businesses that operate out of their address at 5 Bartlett Road. It all started twenty-three years ago when Nantucket Vineyards was founded by Dean and Melissa Long. The Longs joined forces with Randy and Wendy Hudson when they started Cisco Brewers 11 years ago, along with a third partner, Jay Harmon, and now owners of the vineyards and the brewery have added a distillery, where they produce Triple Eight Vodka. The winery is now well established, producing several popular wines, including a red blend called Sailor's Delight. Cisco makes a very popular ale called Whale's Tale, but there is also a great audience for their "Growler," a 64-ounce glass jug that you can take to a beach party. For a fee, you can buy the jug, fill it with your beer of choice, and return for discounted refills whenever you want.

Anyone can take a tour of the brewery, winery, and distillery by calling ahead and making an appointment. The tours are offered every Saturday afternoon at 4 p.m.

This is one of those memorable drinks we found when we were sitting in a bar in Las Vegas—crisp, clean, sweetish, and delicious. We weren't given specific instructions, but allusions, to the method. We think we have it here, and we used Nantucket Triple Eight Vodka to test it out. We now call it, appropriately, the Cisco–tini. Just goes to show that what happens in Vegas doesn't always stay in Vegas.

1 perfectly ripe pineapple, about 4 pounds whole
750 milliliters Triple Eight Vodka

Peel the pineapple and cut it into 2-inch cubes. Place the cubes into a sealable jar and pour the vodka over the pineapple. Let it cure at room temperature for about 10 days. Carefully strain the vodka into a separate container, and take the pineapple and squeeze whatever juice you can extract into a bowl. Cheesecloth is the preferred method. Add the two liquids together and put into a cocktail shaker with ice. Shake, strain, and pour into a martini glass and garnish with a fresh slice of pineapple.

We like to use the Triple Eight Vodka, which comes from Cisco Brewers. It is especially pure and sweet because it uses Nantucket water. It is a very soft, clean, bacteria-free vodka.

Note: The Cisco–tini can be varied by using melon in lieu of pineapple, or a sweet fruit of your choice.

GOOMBAY SMASH

One of our favorite summer indulgences is sitting at the Straight Wharf Bar and having one of their power-packed Goombay Smashes. Many a secret has been revealed after a quaff of this drink, many a story told, always to gales of laughter. This is a happy drink. We don't have the recipe from the Straight Wharf, but we do think this approximates it pretty well.

1 measure triple sec
1 1/2 measure cream of coconut (like Coco Lopez)
3 measures dark rum
5 measures pineapple juice
1 measure fresh lime juice

CONDITION	FORECAST
Stone is wet	Rain
Stone is dry	Not Raining
Shadow on ground....	Sunny
White on top	Snowing
Can't see stone	Foggy
Swinging stone	Windy
Stone jumping up & down ...	Earthqu[ake]
Stone gone	Hurrican[e]
Hooked on nail	Out of Se[ason]

ENJOY YOUR STAY!

This drink evokes images of whaling captains and all that yo-ho-ho. We all have our idea of what this drink should taste like, and on a cold brisk day, it certainly sounds appealing. We have tried dozens of recipes and finally settled on this old Southern version. The nice thing about this is that you can make up the butter sugar mix in batches, store it in your refrigerator in jars or lidded glasses, and give it away at Christmastime. For us, however, it is perfect for those picnics that fall on a cool day, which foretells a chilly evening, or for our end-of-summer picnic. This recipe makes a large quantity, and your personal serving should include 1 tablespoon of the mix to 2 ounces of golden rum and the boiling water, which provides the heat. If you find this mixture too powerful, increase the hot water.

1 pound butter
2 pounds brown sugar
3 eggs
1 teaspoon cinnamon
1/2 teaspoon allspice
1 teaspoon nutmeg
2 ounces rum
2 ounces boiling water

Mix and melt butter and brown sugar. Cool and put into an electric mixer. Add the eggs and the spices and beat until thoroughly incorporated and sugar has broken down. (The original recipe calls for 1 hour of beating, but in a food processor it would certainly be far less.) When ready to serve, find a nice mug, add the rum and 1 tablespoon of mix, add boiling water, and stir.

MADEQUECHAM MARGARITA

Serves 4

Deborah

One summer before we bought out own home, we rented a house called Pike's Peak on the South Shore in Madequecham with our best friends. When we were not watching the planes land at the proximate airport (that was the summer of New York Air's red jets, which was a morning and afternoon sighting event), we were cooking outside and eating at the beach or on the decks. We had a spectacular view of the sunsets, and we celebrated many evenings with these first-rate, absolutely authentic, fresh margaritas.

5 ounces white tequila
4 ounces triple sec
Juice of 2 fresh lemons
Kosher salt
Ice

Place tequila, triple sec, and lemon juice in a shaker and add ice. Rim the edge of four glasses, first with a cut lemon and then with kosher salt. Pour drinks into rimmed glasses and serve. (If you want a frozen margarita, put first three ingredients in blender and frappé.)

MOSCOW MULE

This drink originated in the 1940s and has stood the test of time. Do not substitute ginger ale for ginger beer as it compromises the taste.

4 measures vodka
1 measure fresh-squeezed lime juice
1 measure concentrated sugar syrup
1 dash bitters
2 measures ginger beer

Combine first four ingredients and top with ginger beer.

MANGO AND MALIBU

Serves 8

Deborah

Working in the restaurant business in Rhode Island, I am regularly offered amazing food and drink. This cocktail was served at a press luncheon at one of Providence's premier restaurants, 10 Prime Steak and Sushi; we have amended it slightly and serve it at every summer gathering we have. I used to put my nose up at coconut rum, but after discovering this drink, I am a believer.

1 quart mango juice
1 quart orange juice
1 quart Malibu rum
Mint or tarragon

Mix all ingredients together and serve on ice with a sprig of mint or tarragon.

PIÑA COLADA

Serves 2

Our version of this tropical favorite is made in the blender. It should be energetically shaken at the beach and enthusiastically quaffed once it is poured.

3/4 cup pineapple juice
1/2 cup cream of coconut
8 ounces white rum
1/4 cup heavy cream
4 tablespoons fresh lemon juice
Crushed ice
Lemon zest

Combine first five ingredients in blender and frappé. Pour over crushed ice at the beach and garnish with lemon zest.

NANTUCKET ICED TEA

Serves 6

This drink not only looks like summertime with its vibrant yellow color, but it has a Caribbean island taste with the rum and pineapple. It is the perfect drink for a hot summer's night.

2 tea bags
2 cups boiling water
3 teaspoons brown sugar
1 cup pineapple juice
1/3 cup white rum
2 cups ginger ale or sprite
Fresh pineapple
Ice cubes

In a large saucepan, boil water and add teabags. Remove from heat and let steep for approximately 5–10 minutes. Remove tea bags, stir in brown sugar, and put in refrigerator to chill a bit. Remove from the refrigerator, and stir in pineapple juice and rum. Just before serving, pour the ginger ale into the tea. Put ice cubes in each glass, pour in the tea mixture, and garnish with fresh pineapple.

Serves 8

Picnic regular Mary Jo Beck brought this to one of our picnics 20 years ago, and we are now never without it. It certainly gets the party rolling, and we start serving it as the first beach chair unfolds. Beware—they go down awfully easy, and if you're thirsty at the outset, you may be dizzy before dinner.

1 3/4 quarts of orange juice, chilled
24 ounces pineapple juice, chilled
1 quart dark rum (preferably Myer's), chilled
2 tablespoons freshly squeezed lemon juice
3 dashes bitters
1/4 cup grenadine
Mint sprig for garnish

Mix all ingredients, except mint, in a very large plastic jug. It is best if the mixture can be made up the day before as it seems to improve with age. Garnish each glass with fresh mint.

RASPBERRY WINE PUNCH

Serves 10–12

Carla

I have made this refreshing and light punch for many showers and bridal luncheons. I prefer to use fresh raspberries, if they are available. There is not too much alcohol content, which means everyone can get off the beach quite easily and drive home safely. This punch is usually a big hit with the ladies.

1 lemon, thinly sliced
1 lime, thinly sliced
1/2 cup sugar
1 package frozen raspberries, thawed
1 container of fresh raspberries
1 can frozen pink lemonade, thawed
9 cups cold water
1 bottle dry white wine, chilled
2 bottles (16 ounces) lemon-lime carbonated beverage, chilled

Mix all of the ingredients together and serve in a pretty punch bowl or a nice pitcher.

ROYAL RASPBERRY PUNCH

Serves 8

Carla

As the title of this recipe might suggest, I collected this one while living in England. It was served at an event at the Royal Ascot Races, but I imported it and served it many times in Nantucket at luncheons, tea parties, and showers. It goes down very smoothly, that's for sure.

1/2 cup Chambord or red raspberry liqueur
10 ounces bottled carbonated water, chilled
1 bottle champagne
Mint for garnish

Pour the Chambord and carbonated water into a punch bowl. Gently stir, then slowly add the champagne. Serve over ice in a pretty champagne glass with a garnish of fresh mint.

WHISKEY PUNCH

Serves a crowd

In the fall, whiskey tastes more bracing than rum, but this punch still uses all the fruits, including Nantucket cranberries.

1 quart cranberry juice
2 cups pineapple juice
1 cup orange juice
3 cups Tennessee whiskey
1 quart ginger ale

Combine all ingredients and pour into a bowl with a block of ice. Garnish with fresh cranberries.

Serves 4

Lemonade is always refreshing. The wine with all of this citrus makes for an extra-refreshing sunset cocktail.

1 lemon
2 limes
2 oranges
1/2 cup water
1/2 cup sugar
1 quart Chablis
1 cup sparkling mineral water
2 ounces orange liqueur

Cut a slice from the ends of the fruits to make them stand flat. Reserve fruit and place the end slices in a small saucepan with the water and the sugar. Bring to a boil over medium-high heat, stirring to dissolve the sugar. Reduce the heat and simmer for 3 minutes to make a simple syrup. Remove from the heat and let cool to room temperature. Strain the syrup, squeezing the juices from the fruit. Discard the fruit end slices. Chill the syrup, which may be kept up to one week. When ready to serve, combine the syrup with the Chablis, mineral water, and an orange liqueur. Pour over ice.

This is a scaled-down version of the White Wine Lemonade in that it's much simpler to throw together.

32 ounces lemon-lime soda
1 1-liter bottle dry white wine
1 lemon, thinly sliced
1 lime, thinly sliced
1 tray ice cubes

Mix all ingredients in a plastic jug with lid and add ice. Get to the beach ASAP for a refreshing end-to-the-day drink.

Makes 2 1/2 quarts

During Christmas Stroll, when the air is chilly and the atmosphere festive, Nantucket Town is packed with shoppers and strollers. The tradition is for shopkeepers to offer something back to the people who visit their shops.

At the English Trunk Show Company, we serve this hot cranberry punch. It warms the body and cheers the soul, and nearly everyone asks me for this recipe after having a cup. We also make it for our fall beach picnics, where it is equally appreciated. So, finally, after many requests, I am sharing my secret recipe.

2 cans jellied cranberry sauce
3 cups water
1 cup water
3/4 cup brown sugar
1/4 teaspoon salt
1/4 teaspoon nutmeg
1/2 teaspoon cinnamon
1/2 teaspoon allspice
3/4 teaspoon ground cloves
1 quart pineapple juice

Crush cranberry sauce with a potato masher in a large pot. Add 3 cups of water and beat with an electric mixer until smooth. Add one more cup of water with brown sugar, salt, and spices. Bring to a boil. Add pineapple juice and serve nice and hot.

When summer ends and the island takes on a new beauty, there is still time to have one more picnic. Fall brings many sunny days where winter is a mere hint in the breeze.

For those fall picnics, a lunch on the beach is a great way to say goodbye to friends heading back to the mainland.

Before you store your chairs and tables, head past the red moors of Madaquecham and settle into the dunes and have one more feast of steaming chowder. Bring a pot of chili to the beach and serve it with a big green salad and some garlic-cheese bread you warm on the coals. Use your fire to grill some peaches and serve them with the whipped cream you have in the cooler.

CONCLUSION

Nantucket is in a constant state of change. It seems that it is always being discovered by new people who, like all who have come before, want to make it their own. Everyone would agree that Nantucket was preserved largely because it was ignored. When the old whalers were put out to pasture by new sources of lamp oil, Nantucket sat unchanged for nearly a century.

But those days are long over, and Nantucket property has become as precious a commodity as that old whale oil once was. The old timers will forever lament that what they loved is gone, and indeed, some of it has. Many dear faces are gone, many houses we remember have been replaced with newer models, many restaurants we loved have closed forever. But much of what is precious remains intact—the sand, the sea, the breeze, the flowers, the gentle landscape.

For that, and much, much more, we are grateful, and we will continue to love Nantucket. We love that there is beauty wherever we look. We love that new children are discovering hermit crabs and riding their bikes past the windmill. We love seeing the farm truck on the cobblestones of Main Street. We love seeing the surf before a big storm. We love the moors and the dunes and the weathered gray houses. We love our island, and we appreciate the sights, sounds, smells, tastes, and feel of it, and we cherish the friendships we have made here and the times we have spent together on lovely windswept beaches.

And as long as there is sand and sea, there will be beach picnics and people who want to sit beside the waves and enjoy the total feast of the senses.

Deborah Moxham is a marketing consultant to Rhode Island restaurants. She is the author of *The Grapevine Guide to Rhode Island's Best Restaurants.* Her career began in New York City, where she worked initially as a reporter and writer at Metromedia, then CBS, and, finally, for seven years as a writer and producer for NBC television news. Since moving to Rhode Island, she has worked in production at the local CBS affiliate, written freelance articles, and run a successful business consulting for and marketing local restaurants. Deborah has been very involved with the culinary community in New England for the past 16 years. She created and produced a charity event called Cooks and Books, which brought in major culinary talent, beginning with Julia Child and including many well-known writers and chefs, like Paul Prudhomme, Jacques Pepin, Sheila Lukins, and more. She also designed the Culinary Arts program for Rhode Island School of Design. She has spent much of her life in Nantucket and descends from generations of Nantucket families, going back to the original settlers.

Carla Finn is a longtime friend who shares a deep love of the island and has been visiting and living there for the grater part of her life. After living abroad in England for five years during the 1990's, she returned to the states and opened an antique shop on Nantucket. The English Trunk Show Company, is now in its ninth year. Carla enjoys every aspect of her business but her favorite part is being a member of the Nantucket community and meeting many wonderful and different people on a daily basis. She has loved being the party planner for dozens of events and has hosted hundreds of parties. That experience, plus her extensive knowledge of the island and all its dunes and attractions has been an invaluable part of this book.

Together Debby and Carla have created every kind of picnic from the casual to the fancy and have amassed hundreds of recipes along the way. These recipes are designed for easy al fresco dining, bur rest assured, they will also make an impressive meal at home.

Antipasto Fish Salad 128

Annye's Whole Foods 107

Asian Cole Slaw 57

Asparagus-and Ham Tarts 42

Asparagus-Grilled 140

Asparagus-Sesame 141

Autumn Bisque 38

Balsamic Risotto Salad 55

Barnacle Clam Chowder 39

Beach Blanket Espresso Brownies 166

Beans- Green Beans with Basil Salad 61

Beef

   21 Federal Chili 116

   Moonlight Madness 118

   Surprise Burgers 120

   Moonlight Madness Hangar Steak 118

Beet Soup 40

Berry Streusel French Toast 74

Bill Sandole's East Coast Seafood 131

Bill Sandole's Fish Salad 130

Bloody Mary 193

Blue Cheese and Caramelized Shallot Dip 30

Blue Cheese Mash 145

Bluefish Grilled with Tomato and Fennel 132

Brant Point Brunch 75

Brant Point Butterscotch Thins 180

Bridesmaids' Biscuits 182

Bridesmaids' Lunch 88

Bring on the Baby Cocktail 194

Caipirinha 195

Cakes

    Daffodil Weekend 168

    Fourth of July Firecracker 172

    S'mores 179

    Watermelon 188

Carla's Sand Dollars 43

Cheddar Chili Corn 146

Cheesy Creamy Spinach 149

Chicken

    Cooked Under a Brick 95

    Grilled with Capers and Prunes 98

    Gai Yang 92

    Chutney Chicken Salad 91

    Grilled Breasts with Fresh Tomatoes 96

    Grilled with Capers and Prunes 98

    Rosemary Chicken Salad Sandwiches 86

    Salad Sandwiches with Olive Paste 86

    Sticky with Coconut 99

Chickpea Salad 56

Chile Con Queso 33

Chili - 21 Federal 116

Cisco Brewery 195

Cisco-tini 197

Clam Chowder, Barnacle 39

Clambake - Toddy's Nantucket 126

Clotted Cream 79

Cocktails

Bring on the Baby 194

Caipirinha 195

Madequecham Margarita 200

Mango and Malibu 201

Piña Colada 202

Bloody Mary 193

Cisco-tini 197

Goombay Smash 198

Hot Buttered Rum 199

Raspberry Wine Punch 205

Madaket Mojito 192

Moscow Mule 201

Nantucket Iced Tea 202

Nantucket Planters Punch 204

Royal Raspberry Punch 205

Southsiders 23

Sundown Cooler 208

Whiskey Punch 206

Warm Cranberry Punch 209

White Wine Lemonade 207

Cold Chinese Noodles 58

Cookies

    Bridesmaid's Biscuits 182

    Butterscotch Thins 180

    Ice Cream Sandwiches 175

    Nantucket Blues... 181

    Pink Lemonade... 185

    Rosemary Shortbreads 186

    Texas Goldbars... 187

Corn

    Cheddar Chili... 146

    Grilled with Hot Lime Butter 148

    Perfect... 147

    Ultimate Corn Salad 67

Crabmeat and Egg Lasagna....................................... 76

Cream Cheese and Date Sandwiches 81

Cream Cheese Crescents 44

Crispy Fish with Lemon 129

Cucumber Sandwiches 83

Curried Rice 158

Daffodil Weekend Cake... 168

Daisy's Dip.. 31

Dinner with the Banshees.. 103

Dip

    Shrimp 36

Sweet Coconut 37

Blue Cheese and Caramelized Onion 30

Warm Cheddar and Onion.. 32

Daisy's.. 31

Pineapple Curry 35

Duck-Grilled with Asian Marinade 104

Easy Pepper Relish 12

Egg Salad Sandwiches.. 84

Figs with Prosciutto and Blue Cheese............................ 45

Fish-Antipasto 128

Fourth of July Blueberry Pie 171

Fourth of July Firecracker Cakes.................................. 172

French Potato Salad with Fines Herbes 60

Goombay Smash 198

Green Bean and Basil Salad 61

Green Beans and Garlic Packet 161

Green Salad with Avocado and Citrus Dressing 62

Grilled Asparagus 140

Grilled Bluefish with Tomato and Fennel 132

Grilled Chicken with Capers and Prunes 98

Grilled Chicken with Fresh Tomatoes 96

Grilled Corn 148

Grilled Duck Breast with Asian Marinade 104

Grilled Marinated Shrimp... 135

Grilled Meatloaf 105

Grilled Oysters 134

Grilled Peaches 174

Grilled Potatoes with Blue Cheese and Scallion 150

Grilled Roasted Fish with Cucumber Sauce...................... 133

Grilled Sausage with Cheddar and Onions 46

Grilled Summer Vegetables 152

Grilled Tomatoes 154

Ham Rolls 47

Hearty Egg and Bacon Brunch 79

Heirloom Tomato Pie 90

Hot Buttered Rum 199

Ice Cream Sandwiches 175

Island Tea Sandwiches 85

Italian Zucchini Pie 89

Jerusalem Artichoke Soup 41

Lamb and White Bean Salad.. 115

Lamb Burgers with Feta and Onions 114

Lamb-Butterflied #1 112

Lamb-Butterflied #2 113

Madaket Mojito 192

Madequecham Margarita... 200

Mango and Malibu 201

Marinated Mushrooms 161

Marscapone and Meringues 167

Martini Salmon 137

Michael's Mushroom in Honor of Sydney 142

Moonlight Madness 118

Moscow Mule 201

Mushroom-with sauce a la Shannon 142

Nantucket Beach Bread 48

Nantucket Blues 181

Nantucket Iced Tea 202

Nantucket Planters Punch 204

Onions-Balsamic Red 153

Orange Poppy Seed Salad 63

Orange Rasberry Ambrosia 177

Orange Rosemary Pork Chops 106

Packets

    Summer Vegetable 162

    Green Beans and Garlic 161

    Marinated Mushroom 161

    Sweet Potato 160

    Tomatoes and Shallots 162

Pasta with Black Olive Pesto 144

Perfect Corn 147

Pies - Fourth of July Blueberry Pie 171

Pina Colada 202

Pineapple Curry Dip 35

Pink Lemonade Cookies 185

Pork

    Dinner with the Banshees 103

    Orange Rosemary Chops 106

    Sweet and Sour Pork Tenderloins 109

Sweet and Spicy Pork Tenderloins 110

Potatoes

Blue Cheese Mash 145

Grilled with Blue Cheese and Scallion 150

French Potato Salad 60

Potatoes Anna 151

Raspberry Wine Punch 205

Red Pepper Relish 120

Red Peppers- Roasted and Stuffed 163

Rice-Curried 158

Rice-Tex Mex 159

Riding-out-the-Storm Macaroni and Cheese 24

Roasted Stuffed Peppers 163

Rosemary Chicken Salad Tea Sandwiches 86

Rosemary Shortbread Cookies 186

Royal Raspberry Punch 206

Roy's Roasted Vidalia Onions 153

Salads

Thai Cucumber 65

Chutney Chicken 91

Green with Avocado and Citrus Dressing 62

Asian Cole Slaw 57

Balsamic Risotto 55

Chickpea 56

Cold Chinese Noodles 58

French Potato with Fines Herbes 60

Fruit Salad with Lime Marinade 59

Green Bean and Basil 61

Lamb and White Bean 115

Orange Poppy Seed 63

Spinach with Apricot Vinaigrette 64

Summer Beet 66

Turkey Tostada.. 101

Ultimate Corn 67

Watermelon 69

White Bean 70

Salmon

Martini 137

Grilled with Cucumber Dill Sauce 133

Crispy with Lemon 129

Sandwiches

Chicken Salad with Olive Paste 82

Cream Cheese and Date.. 81

Cucumber 83

Egg Salad 84

Island Tea... 85

Rosemary Chicken Salad 86

Watercress and Stilton.. 80

Sausage, Grilled with Cheddar and Onions 46

Sesame Asparagus 141

Shrimp - Grilled Marinated 135

Shrimp Dip.. 36

Smoked Bluefish Pate 49

Smoky Babaganoush 34

S'mores Cake 179

Soup

    Autumn Bisque 38

    Roasted Beet 40

    Clam Chowder 39

    Jerusalem Artichoke Soup 41

Southwestern Pumpkin-Seed Quesadillas 51

Spanakopita Pie 157

Spinach Salad with Apricot Vinaigrette 64

Spinach-Cheesy Creamy 149

Spinach-Spanakopita Pie 157

Spinach-Tomato Pie 155

Stuffed Tomatoes 156

Summer Beet Salad 66

Summer Plum Blueberry Nectarine Cobbler 176

Summer Vegetable Packet 162

Surprise Burgers 120

Sweet-and-Sour Pork Tenderloins 109

Sweet-and-Spicy Pork Tenderloins 110

Sweet Coconut Dip 37

Sweet Potato Packet 160

Swordfish Marinade 136

Teriyaki Chicken Burgers 100

Teriyaki Marinade.. 123

Tex-Mex Rice.. 159

Texas Gold Bars... 187

Thai Cucumber Salad 65

Toddy's Nntucket Clambake 126

Tomato Spinach Pie... 155

Tomatoes and Shallots Packet 162

Tomatoes- grilled.. 154

Tomato-Heirloom Pie 90

Tomato-Spinach Pie 155

True English Scones 77

Turkey Tostada Salad 101

Ultimate Corn Salad... 67

Veal Chops with Herb Butters 121

Vidalia Onions, Roasted on the Grill 153

Warm Cheddar and Onion Dip...................................... 32

Warm Cranberry Punch.. 209

Watercress and Stilton Sandwiches 80

Watermelon Cake... 188

White Bean Salad 70